WARBIRD TECH
SERIES

VOLUME 11

NORTH AMERICAN
NA-16/AT-6/SNJ

By Dan Hagedorn

specialtypress
PUBLISHERS AND WHOLESALERS

Copyright © 1997 Dan Hagedorn

Published by
Specialty Press Publishers and Wholesalers
11481 Kost Dam Road
North Branch, MN 55056
United States of America
(612) 583-3239

Distributed in the UK and Europe by
Airlife Publishing Ltd.
101 Longden Road
Shrewsbury
SY3 9EB
England

ISBN 0-933424-84-1

All rights reserved. No part of this book may be reproduced or transmitted in any form or by any means, electronic or mechanical including photocopying, recording or by any information storage and retrieval system, without permission from the Publisher in writing.

Material contained in this book is intended for historical and entertainment value only, and is not to be construed as usable for aircraft or component restoration, maintenance or use.

Designed by Greg Compton

Printed in the United States of America

TABLE OF CONTENTS

THE NORTH AMERICAN NA-16/AT-6/SNJ

PREFACE **4**

ACKNOWLEDGING THOSE WHO MADE IT ALL POSSIBLE

CHAPTER 1: THE TEXAN DEFINED **6**

AN AIRCRAFT FOR ALL SEASONS

CHAPTER 2: TEXAN ANCESTORS **8**

PRE-AT-6 VARIANTS

CHAPTER 3: DESIGN MATURITY **46**

THE AT-6 AND WORLD WAR TWO VARIANTS

SPECIAL FULL COLOR SECTION: A WORLD OF COLOR **65**

THE TEXAN SERIES PROVIDES INFINITE COLOR AND MARKING VARIATIONS

CHAPTER 4: POST-WAR VARIANTS **80**

FINAL REFINEMENTS AND A NEW LEASE ON LIFE

SIGNIFICANT DATES **100**

KEY DATES IN THE HISTORY OF THE NA-16/AT-6/SNJ

WARBIRDTECH
SERIES

PREFACE

ACKNOWLEDGING THOSE WHO MADE IT ALL POSSIBLE

For readers familiar with my previous works, which for many years have focused on the airplane and its use in Latin America, this book on the details of the North American NA-16, AT-6, SNJ Texan and Harvard lineage may at first blush appear to be a departure from the fold.

However, the history of the NA-16 family of aircraft, from original concept through the end of the line, is inextricably linked to Latin America. Much of the early export success achieved by the series, which enabled North American to prosper and move on to other developments, is owed to the sales made in starts and spurts to export customers, a sizeable quantity of which were to Latin America.

Besides these historical antecedents, however, I must confess to a life-long love affair with this absolutely astonishing series of airplanes, and when asked, I unashamedly admit that they are collectively, hands-down, my all-time favorites.

This book, part of the innovative new Specialty Press series, offers you a look at the AT-6 series that has not previously been available between two covers. And while it is customary to praise and give thanks to the legions of fellow enthusiasts who unselfishly gave of their time, talents, collections and critical review, this is also the place to pass along kudos to some folks who seldom get any press whatsoever.

Therefore, thanks first and foremost to the North American employees, managers and designers who lived during the mid-1930s and literally breathed life into what has become unquestionably the best piston-engined military training aircraft of all time. Thanks to the draftsmen and unnamed NAA workers who caused the engineering drawings to be skillfully and beautifully prepared, and for USAF's wisdom in seeing that they were preserved on microfilm. I felt obliged to review these drawings in preparation for this book, and you will find selected examples in these pages.

Thanks also to similar teams who prepared the vital manuals, reports and Technical Orders, which dictated the day-to-day service lives of the airplanes and are an absolute gold mine of historical detail. Excerpts from these also appear in these pages.

Two other special collections I consulted in preparing this book also deserve mention, in addition to the works noted below. These are the little-known Sarah Clark Collection held at the National Archives at College Park, Maryland, and the Wright Field Technical Documents Library Collection, held by the Archives Division of the National Air and Space Museum at Silver Hill, Maryland. These collections provided me with invaluable correspondence and reports that proved to be virtually a paper trail of the teething problems, experimental work and fielding of the NA-16 series in the U.S. Armed Forces, as well as overseas. The folks at College Park, especially the Military Textual Reference Staff, went out of their way to guide me through the huge Clark Collection, while the

A virtually brand-new BC-1A is part of a California National Guard unit at Oakland in July 1941. (Peter M. Bowers)

incomparable Larry Wilson, co-worker and friend, led me through the intricacies of the Wright Field Collection.

Using the resources of the Library of Congress, the National Air and Space Museum Branch Library, the National Archives, and the Archives of the National Air and Space Museum (be it noted, on my own time), I have made a concerted attempt to review everything that has been printed on the NA-16, AT-6, SNJ and Harvard series. There are a surprising number of books on these aircraft and a truly dizzying group of magazine articles. The very best of the books, in my opinion, included the following: *The Harvard File*, compiled by John F. Hamlin (An Air-Britain Publication, London, 1988, ISBN 0-85130-160-6); *T-6 Texan in Action, Aircraft Number 94,* by Larry Davis (Squadron/Signal Publications, 1989, ISBN 0-89747-224-1); *The Incredible T-6 Pilot Maker*, by Walt Ohlrich and Jeff Ethell (Specialty Press, 1983, ISBN 0-933424-34-5); *T-6, A Pictorial Record of the Harvard, Texan and Wirraway*, by Peter C. Smith, (Motorbooks International, 1995, ISBN 0-7603-0191-3). I found two periodical citations of particular value. The first was Colonel John A. deVries article "North American AT-6/SNJ Texan" that appeared in *Historical Aviation Album* in 1979. In my opinion, the absolute best article ever done on the series was Peter M. Bowers'

The 251 BT-14 (NA-58) basic trainers acquired by the USAAC are probably the easiest variant of the NA-16 to pick out of a lineup. The only exception is the similar (and solitary) BT-9D, the BT-14's sire. Their rather graceful forward slope down to the engine cowl was unique in the entire series. (USAAC)

two-part series in *Wings/Airpower* some years ago entitled "Riding Herd on the Thundering Texan."

My goal was to present for your enjoyment as many unpublished images of the NA-16 series as possible, and I took considerable trouble to ensure that this was achieved. This would have been impossible, however, without the selfless contributions of the likes of Robert F. Dorr, who sent a batch of glossies from his wonderful collection within days of the announcement of this project; my dear friend Dave Ostrowski, editor of *Skyways* magazine, who continuously astounded me with the depth of his black and white negative collections; and Peter M. Bowers, who provided more than 30 of his priceless negatives to a guy who was reading his work when he was a teenager!

Thanks also to Warren Bodie, one of the finest aviation photographers on earth and an aerohistorian with a unique point of view, as well as the underpaid, overworked, and seldom appreciated youngsters at the Still Pictures Branch of the National Archives. While they may not have known the difference between an AT-6 and a Piper J-3 at the outset, they tried their best to help me locate some of the gems in these pages. Ray Wagner, a San Diego Aerospace Museum Archivist, provided several exceptionally rare photos from the collections of that outstanding facility, and Leo Kohn, an aerohistorian who seldom gets the praise he deserves, contributed many photos from his personal files that have never been published before. Friend Leif Hellström and Lennart Andersson helped keep me straight on the Swedish NA-16 variants and clarified several long-standing myths, as did Peter Liander.

Sincere thanks also to Phil Edwards of the NASM Branch Library staff, and Hal Andrews, Naval Historian Emeritus, for his unequaled insights and feedback. Friend Bob Esposito contributed several rare photos from his excellent collection and really came through in the crunch.

Finally, my thanks and love to my sweetheart and wife, Kathleen, who has endured my love of aviation and allowed me to share that part of myself with others.

DAN HAGEDORN
1997

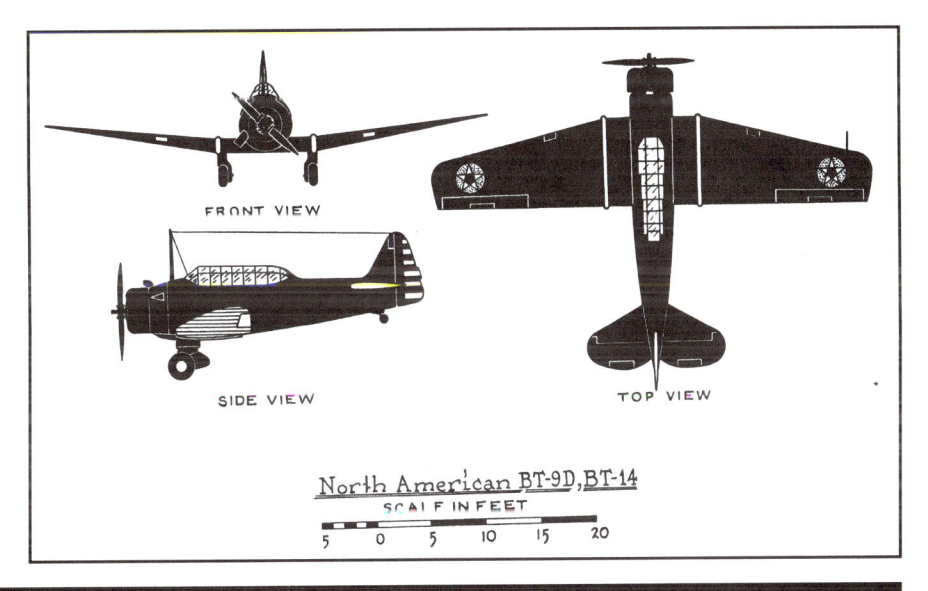

THE TEXAN DEFINED

AN AIRCRAFT FOR ALL SEASONS

At a small, friendly Antique Airplane Association fly-in in Cambridge, Maryland, some years ago, my wife first became acquainted with the Texan. Her introduction to the aircraft was probably similar to that of many, many others over the years.

In fact, the aircraft in question was a beautifully restored SNJ-4, a Navy version of the series, and my bride had not failed to notice the attention I had lavished on it, the obvious king of the roost among the nattering Piper Cubs, Stearman biplanes and lesser classics that inhabited the small field that weekend. Smiling to myself, gently touching the gleaming blue body and wings here and there, Kathleen sensed that here, indeed, was a rival for my attentions to be reckoned with.

As the gathering wound down, however, and the friendly pilots and their ladies started putting their lawn chairs and detritus away for the trips home, we slowly backed away from the beautiful Texan as it became clear that her owner was about to crank up the engine. When it finally came to life, Kathleen looked at me, consternation on her face, and shouted "What's *wrong* with that aircraft?!" She had heard the voice of the Texan—music to mine ears—for the very first time, an experience I had rather forgotten.

That sound, and the sound at take-off and fly-past, speaks volumes about this aircraft and the entire, long-lived series that began with the first NA-16. Much has been written extolling the virtues of the AT-6 series and while they are invariably true and bear frequent repeating, allow me to leave you with your first memory of the sound of the aircraft, as this account is intended to bring you something more than just one more testimonial to the breed. If you haven't had that memory yet, by all means attend virtually any air show, anywhere, and experience it.

The NA-16 and Texan family history can be rather crudely segmented into four major epochs, from both the manufacturer's standpoint and, conveniently, from a historical perspective. These consisted of (1) those built (or license-built) for export to foreign operators and had no U.S. service connections; (2) those built as new aircraft, at least at the outset, for the U.S. Armed Forces exclusively; (3) those built under U.S. Armed Forces funding specifically for use by Allied nations under the provisions of the Defense Aid programs and Lend-Lease during World War Two; and (4) those remanufactured, modernized, reconfigured or license-built for post-World War Two use by the U.S. Armed Forces and foreign operators. Aside from civil-registered Texans bought surplus after the end of World War Two and since, all that follows in this volume fits somewhere in one or more combinations of these four epochs.

During my extensive research, a number of interesting facts emerged. One of the most glaring of these is that no two sources quoted the same total for NA-16 and Texan aircraft built! By the time you have finished this type-by-type survey, it will become apparent why it may be impossible to arrive at such a once-and-for-all grand total. Some of the grand totals cited in otherwise respectable works on the aircraft vary by as much as 1,500 to 2,000 airframes, while the smallest variation total was in the neighborhood of 350 airframes. *The USAAF World War Two Statistical Digest,* for example, lists a grand total of 15,094 AT-6s of all variants acquired between January 1940 and August 1945. However, actual acceptances by the USAAF from the factories during the calendar years of the war reflect a total of only 14,130, as follows:

INGLEWOOD DELIVERIES

1940	*1941*	*1942*
631	1524	8

DALLAS DELIVERIES

1941	*1942*	*1943*	*1944*	*1945*
711	3,697	4,024	3,298	1,237

Confusing the issue are the approximately 13,511 accidents suffered by USAAF Advanced Training aircraft during the war, resulting in the loss of not fewer than 2,227 AT types, a sizeable number of which must have been AT-6 variants.

This disparity in the totals built (and lost to various causes) is well-illustrated by one batch of 68 aircraft in particular, which are described here for the first time in detail anywhere in public print. U.S. Air Force serial numbers 48-1301 to 48-1368 were a batch of rebuilt aircraft—24 ex-U.S. Navy, some ex-USAAF and some assorted surplus aircraft re-purchased by the manufacturer—which were issued the convenience designation of AT-6C, and later became just T-6C. Needless to say, these have never figured in the totals for standard wartime AT-6C production before.

Foreign production of North American NA-16 variants has also been poorly documented, and as a consequence contributed to the incredible disparity in the claims for totals built. It often boiled down to a matter of what it was thought fair to count. Apparently, the USAAF counted some aircraft built on Army contracts and supplied to foreign nations under Lend-Lease, and not others. These are but two examples; many others are found scattered throughout this account.

This study of the NA-16 and Texan series is based to a certain extent on what is often cited as the North American Aviation *O Report*, which lists in roughly chronological order and by NAA designation and Charge Number, all aircraft assigned a North American designation or Charge Number. However, this document is not without errors itself. My primary objective has been to provide basic data about the individual variants, how they differ from earlier and succeeding variants, their manufacturer's serial numbers, user identifications and specific facts about the service lives of the variants. This data will be complimented by previously unpublished photographs showing the exact variant under discussion, as well as detailed drawings of significant or unusual components of the variant.

While Peter M. Bowers did a masterful job of describing the hitherto confusing history of the North American NA-16 series designations and Charge Numbers in his *Wings/Airpower* two-part series, described earlier, he did not have access to intelligence documents which conclusively demonstrated that, in spite of the NAA designation system, the host countries almost invariably referred to the aircraft they received by the Charge Number rather than by the NAA designation. In U.S. State Department Export License Authorizations, U.S. Order of Battle documents and U.S. Mission Reports, Brazil's NA-44s, for example, were nearly always cited as NA-72s (the Charge Number) rather than the NAA designation (NA-44), while the 50 AT-6Bs supplied to Latin American nations in the early months of 1942 by Presidential order are often cited in local documents as NA-84s.

Basically, North American designations for the NA-16 series fell into one of the five ranges. These broad descriptions are extracted directly from NAA marketing literature of the late 1930s:

- **NA-16-1 General Purpose Two-place** offered with a 550HP Pratt & Whitney S3H1 Wasp engine;

- **NA-16-2 Fighter Two-place** offered with the 500HP Pratt & Whitney S6H1 Wasp engine;

- **NA-16-3 Bomber Two-place** offered with the 500HP Pratt & Whitney S6H1 Wasp engine;

- **NA-16-4 Advanced Trainer Two-place** offered with the 440HP Wright R-975-E3 engine; and

- **NA-16-5 Fighter Single-place** offered with the 835HP Wright SR-1820G-37 engine.

Seldom mentioned, but invariably included as a footnote in NAA marketing literature (in several languages) of the period, was that "any of the above airplanes may be equipped with float type landing gear," although there are no recorded instances where any customer took up this interesting option.

Each customer was given a separate NAA number, based on the above five broad groupings, for the aircraft on his order, even though it often duplicated the designation of another customer. For engineering and accounting office reasons, however, there were Charge Numbers that, eventually, became more definitive than the NAA designation system had ever been. When China and the Brazilian Navy both opted for what NAA termed NA-16-4s, for example, NAA Charge Numbers and Contracts read NA-41 and NA-46, while a follow-on Chinese order for essentially identical NA-16-4s were identified by the Charge Number NA-56. You will quickly recognize the value of these numbers, as apparently, did the customers.

At first glance it may appear that this survey leans heavily towards the "numbers basher," but the value of precision in defining aircraft in this series will, hopefully, become apparent. For some readers, this will be the first type-by-type description they have ever read. Hopefully, the information presented will stimulate further research into the questions yet remaining.

TEXAN ANCESTORS

PRE AT-6 VARIANTS

NA-16

NAA DESIGNATION:	NA-16
NAA CHARGE NUMBER:	NA-16
MFG. S/N:	NA-16-1
USER REGN. OR S/N:	X-2080

The Granddaddy of them all, the first NA-16, was identified by North American as "a two-place basic trainer demonstrator, open cockpit, fixed gear."

Several reputable sources have stated that the aircraft was initially designated as the GA-16. At the time of design and initial fabrication, the design and manufacturing teams were still at Dundalk, Maryland, operating under the General Aviation Corporation, which was the precursor of North American Aviation. However, available NAA and Civil Aeronautics Administration documents do not bear this out, although the aircraft may have borne the GA-16 designation during its earliest preliminary design stages. Once metal was cut, the aircraft appears to have been referred to strictly as the NA-16 from that point on.

Other sources have stated that the NA-16 was designed specifically for the U.S. Army Air Corps Basic Trainer Competition of 1935. While this was unquestionably a major marketing goal for the NA-16, company literature makes it clear that NAA was equally interested in the emerging and lucrative export market, and it may be more accurate to say that the NA-16 emerged at just the right juncture to take advantage of both opportunities.

The NA-16 was the brainchild of J. H. "Dutch" Kindelberger, J. L. Atwood and H. R. Raynor, based on a crude sketch (reproduced here), which NAA described as "a historical document in the annals of North American." Kindelberger and Atwood left Douglas to join NAA in July 1934, and the NA-16 is reputed to have been designed and built in something like nine weeks, so the first

The Granddaddy of them all, the original North American NA-16 is shown in its initial configuration, probably at Dundalk, Maryland, in April or May 1935. The lines of the breed are clearly evident, even at this nascent stage. The aircraft is reported to have been painted in period USAAC scheme, i.e., blue fuselage and yellow wings and horizontal tail surfaces. (Peter M. Bowers)

Contrary to many accounts, when the NA-16 was evaluated at Wright Field for the famous Basic Trainer Competition in early June 1935, it did have a canopy greenhouse, as shown here. Indeed, this photo, taken April 18, 1935, barely two weeks after the alleged first-flight of the open cockpit original configuration, seems to prove that the canopy was an early modification rather than a later one. The wings, rudder and vertical fin appear to have been painted at this point, possibly yellow. (North American 20.101/120)

WARBIRDTECH SERIES

According to North American (Rockwell) these doodles represent the first conception of the NA-16, in the hand of Kindelberger, Atwood and H. R. Raynor. Even at this stage, a canopy "greenhouse" was in mind. (Rockwell International)

flight on April 1, 1935, with Eddie Allen at the controls at Dundalk gives some measure of the gestation period of the design.

Contrary to popular misconceptions, however, the original, open-cockpit NA-16 was not the configuration tested in the Basic Trainer Competition at Wright Field. The official Air Corps Engineering Section Memorandum Report, Serial Number 4110 dated May 27, 1935, entitled "Performance Test of North American Aviation Basic Training Airplane NA-16, Ident. No. X-2080," definitely describes the aircraft with the "cockpit cabins closed."

The test report revealed that the NA-16 achieved a high speed at sea level of 172MPH and an operating speed of 151.5MPH, while fuel consumption at 1,950RPM at 2,200 feet with mixture control set at "best economy" (for a drop of 50RPM) was 18 gals./hour. This translated to a range of 758 miles. The aircraft had a Wright R-975E-3 engine during these tests.

Although the NA-16 is often cited as having won the Basic Trainer contest with a subsequent order for BT-9s, the other competitors in the competition, the Curtiss-Wright 19R and Seversky SEV-3XAR, were decidedly superior in every measurable category over the NA-16 and were far more advanced designs. Indeed, the Seversky design won a contract for 30 BT-8s, which was the first USAAC

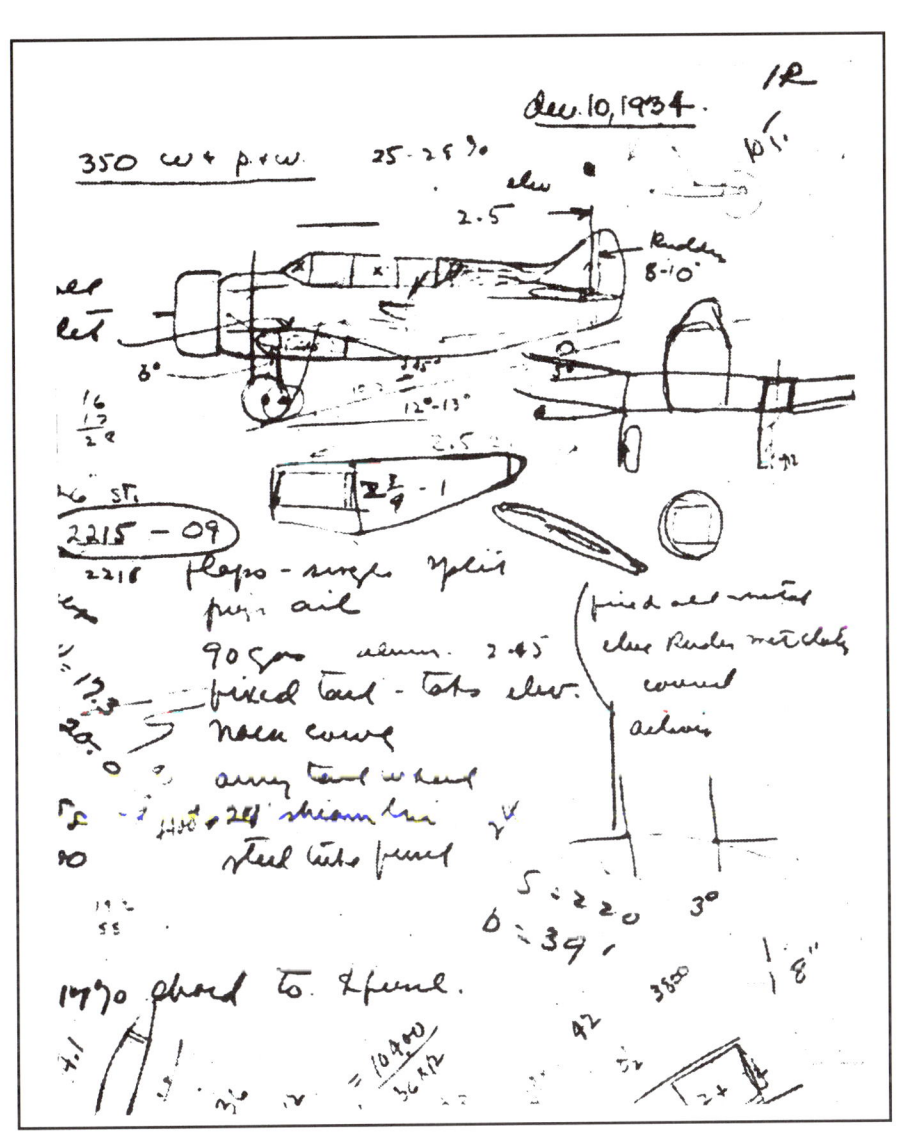

The original NA-16 as tested at Wright Field, Ohio, in competition with the Seversky SEV-3XAR and Curtiss-Wright 19R. (Wright Field Photo No. 51895 via David W. Ostrowski)

After the Wright Field competition, NAA almost immediately commenced grooming the NA-16 for export marketing. In this photo, taken in Maryland, an engine change has been made, twin .30-caliber guns provided for over the nose, and the rear cockpit coaming has been deepened to enhance the gunner's field of fire. Officially, the aircraft was now the NA-18, as shown in the August 26, 1935 view. The color scheme also appears to have been modified from that worn at Wright Field. (A.U. Schmidt Collection via Peter M. Bowers)

Comparing this Maryland locale photo with the similar pose taken at the Wright Field competition reveals that the NA-16 had, by this point, besides the addition of twin nose guns and rear pit modifications, received a completely different engine and a different prop, as well as a modified pitot tube. (via Robert Esposito)

design specifically conceived as a Basic Trainer, ahead of the BT-9. It is probably correct to say that the BT-9 order that followed was due more to the political clout of General Motors (NAA's corporate parent) than to the qualities of the aircraft that flew at Wright Field.

The NA-16 lived on, however, and transmorphed into the next important variant, the NA-18, shortly after the Wright Field trials.

Concurrent with the Air Corps Basic Trainer competition, North American launched a first-class export sales campaign, and even at this early stage, was thinking retractable landing gear variants, although the first of these was still some time to come. (North American)

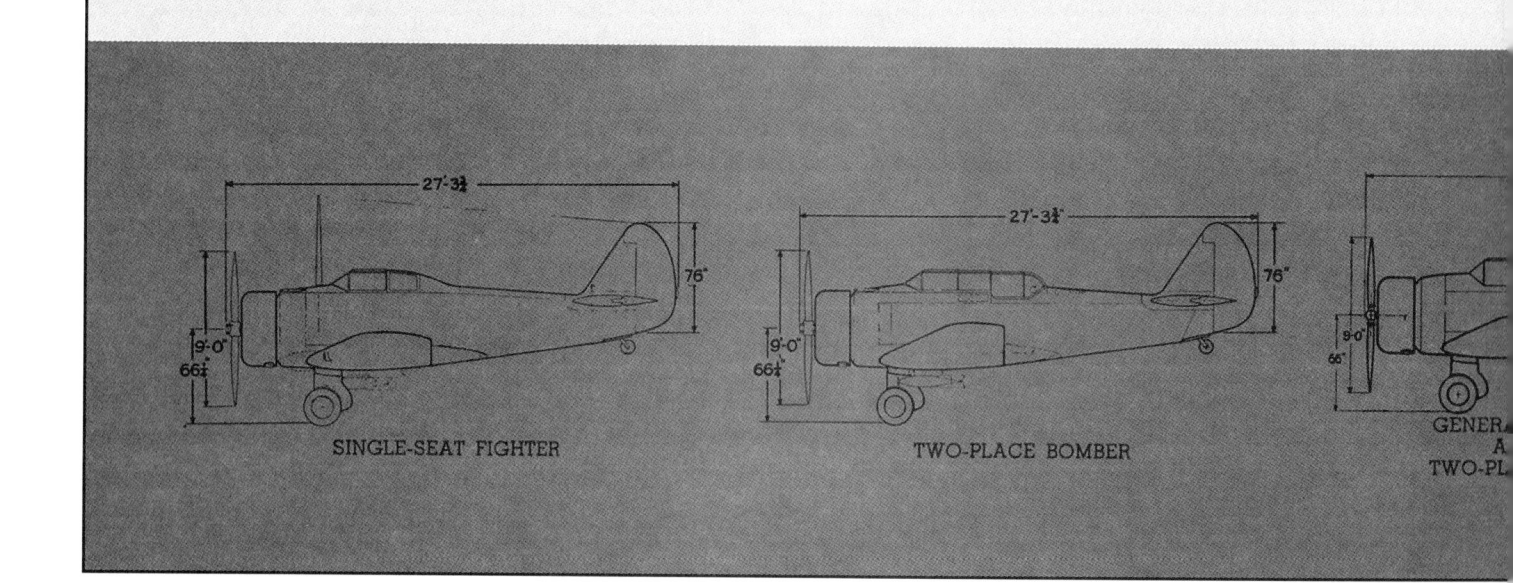

SINGLE-SEAT FIGHTER   TWO-PLACE BOMBER   GENER... TWO-PL...

10

WARBIRDTECH
SERIES

NA-18

NAA Designation:	NA-18
NAA Charge Number:	NA-18
Mfg. S/N:	NA-18-1
User Regn. or S/N:	X-2080, NC-2080 Argentine Army E.a.-301

While NAA was engaging the Army Air Corps in trials of its NA-16 at Wright Field, they were busy arranging their first sales tour of an NA-16 demonstrator development.

This was none other than the original NA-16 (Mfg. S/N NA-16-1), which was hastily modified at the Dundalk factory into at least three distinctly different configurations, the earliest known drawings for which were dated June 27, 1935. Since the aircraft was eventually sold to Argentina in 1937 on Contract AE-43 while allegedly bearing commercial registration NC-2080, the CAA file on X/NC-2080 was destroyed by the National Archives when all of the Export Certificate of Airworthiness files were trashed during the 1970s. We may never know exactly how many or which modifications were made to this aircraft, nor its demonstration contributions to the subsequent success of the NA-16 series, which seem to have been considerable. I find it particularly significant, from a historical perspective, that this pivotal aircraft ended its days in Latin America.

The NA-16/NA-18 was the only aircraft in the entire series manufactured in Maryland, the remainder were built

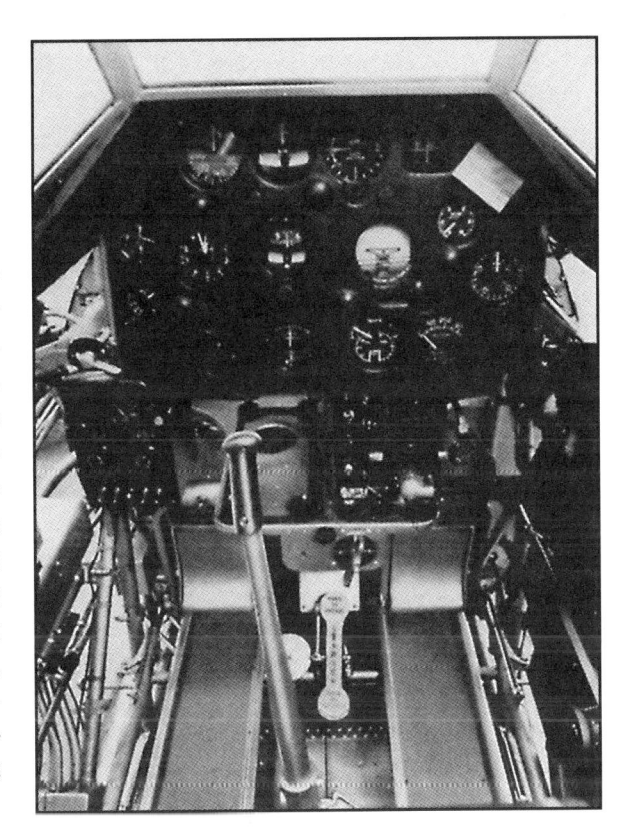

The original "front office" of the NA-16 as offered for export in the NA-18. Customers could customize the front and rear cockpit instrumentation. Rear pits had "easily removable control sticks." (North American)

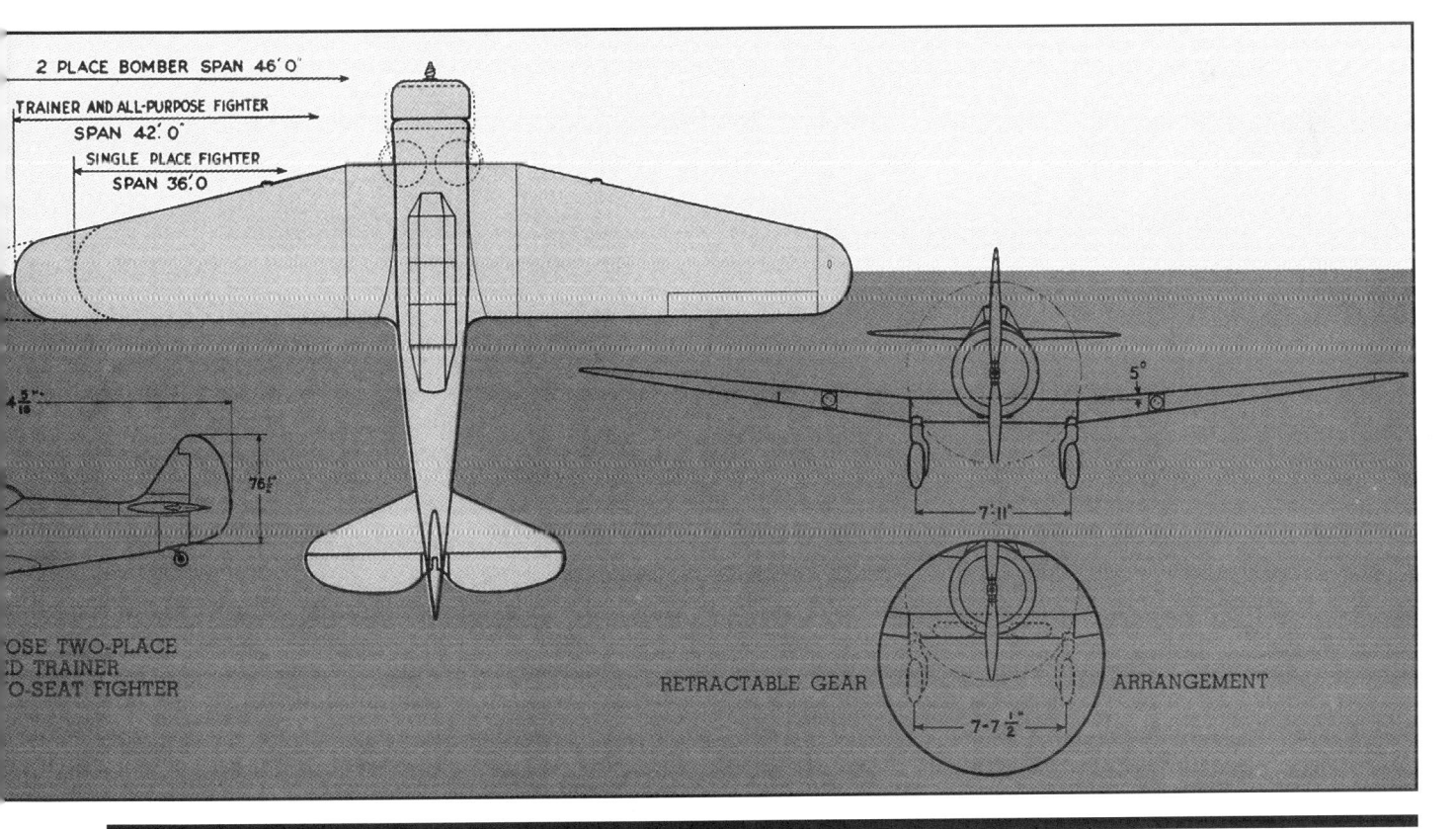

Rear gun installation of the NA-16 configuration is shown as tested at Wright Field, but by the time this August 26, 1935, image was taken the aircraft was called the NA-18. The range of movement was later improved even further on actual export models. Many subsequent NA-16 descendants could mount a .30-caliber free gun in the rear cockpit on a variety of mounts. (North American)

Shown is a close-up view of the rear canopy installation and a stowed .30-caliber gun on the NA-18 X-2080 as of August, 1935. (North American)

The business-end of the export, armed configuration of the NA-16-2 two-place fighter or NA-16-3 two-place bomber version (although the aircraft shown here is actually the solitary NA-18), shows the off-set sight and two .30-caliber guns. A considerable number of export aircraft were built to this configuration, with some variation in the placement of the guns and sight. This aircraft was sold to Argentina in October 1935, minus engine and prop. (North American)

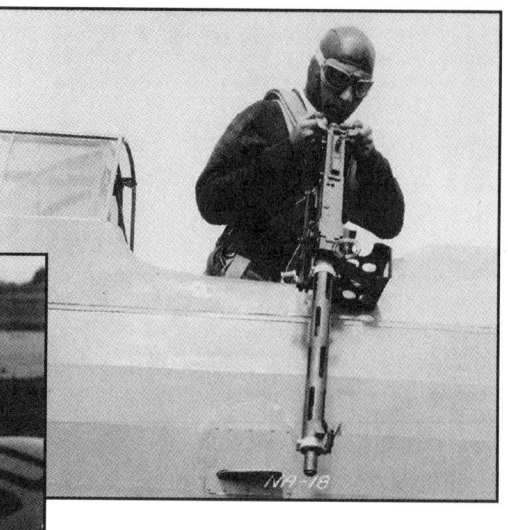

in California, Texas or elsewhere under license. Among other changes, the NA-18 had the earlier 400HP Whirlwind replaced with a 550HP Pratt & Whitney Wasp engine before its sale to Argentina.

NA-19 (BT-9)

NAA DESIGNATION:	NA-19
NAA CHARGE NUMBER:	NA-19
MFG. S/N:	NA-19-1, 3, 5 to 11, 20 to 34, 50 to 67
USER REGN. OR S/N:	36-28 to 36-69

The NAA Charge Number for the 42 BT-9s ordered by the U.S. Army Air Corps was dated October 3, 1935, under contract AC-7881. It called for aircraft fitted with the Wright R-975-7 400HP Whirlwind, which was the Air Corps designation for the R-975-E2T. These BT-9s were superficially similar to the NA-18 and NA-16 as tested at Wright Field, but had considerably wider cockpit areas with differing canopy enclosures and Air Corps cockpit instrumentation. They retained the much-touted fabric-covered fuselage "to ease maintenance" but had metal-covered wings and fixed tail surfaces.

Advances in aircraft technology, training of maintenance personnel

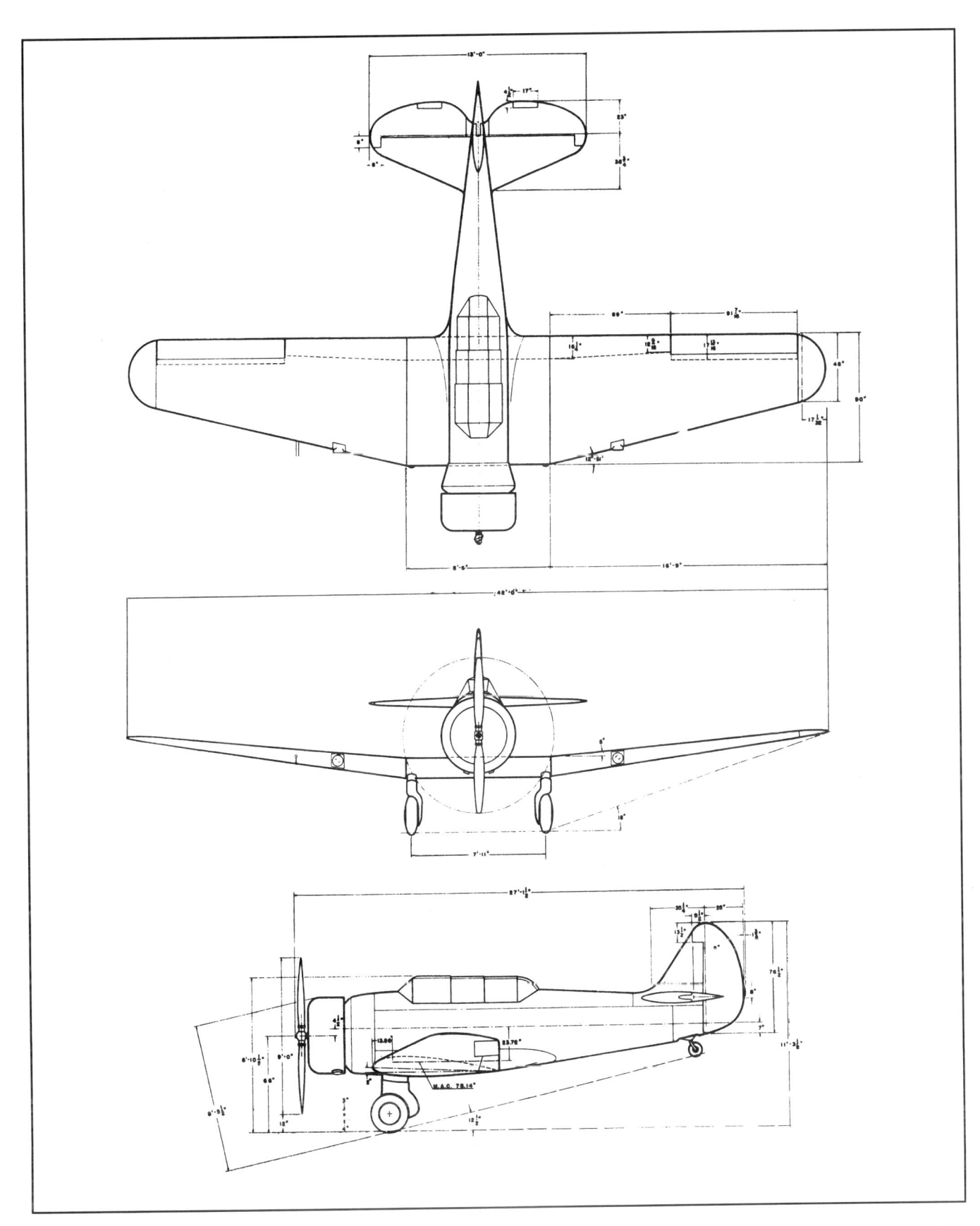

This North American three-view of the NA-18 is dated June 27, 1935, proving that North American wasted no time in moving on to export versions. Interestingly, this drawing does not include the armament provisions or cut-down rear cockpit coaming as reflected on the preceding photos dated August 1935. (North American)

The first Air Corps BT-9 (NA-19) had the rather low-profile canopy of the NA-18, but the curved-down aft portion was faired neatly into the rear turtledeck, since it did not have rear-gun capability, nor any other armament. (Cooke via Peter M. Bowers)

A perfect three-point landing, and a common pose for BT-9s at Randolph Field, Texas. Field Number 267 just shows the leading edge slats, the subject of considerable controversy, and its pre-war colors in this classic view. (David W. Ostrowski)

The front office of Air Corps BT-9 S/N 36-54 is as it was laid out while at Randolph Field in November 1938. Some slight changes had been made since the initial configuration. Note the stenciled "Call 6054" on the lower right side of the panel. (USAF 19259AC via National Archives)

and time eventually caught up with the fabric covered fuselage of the surviving BT-9s. Technical Order 01-6051, dated March 15, 1941, instructed that the fuselage fabric areas on all surviving BT-9s be replaced by "metal-covered side panel spares" as they became available.

As mentioned in a number of other sources, the BT-9 also suffered from rather unfortunate wing tip stall characteristics, which resulted in the addition of slats to the outboard leading edges of the wings. Despite these additions, however, Unsatisfactory Reports (U/Rs) continued to roll in to Wright Field from units and bases that were using these BT-9s. A U/R dated January 4, 1943, stated that "considerable trouble has been experienced at Randolph Field with the installation of stall control strips (Part 40A1277-3) on BT-9 series aircraft." Randolph engineering officials requested permission to replace these, which were apparently interim solutions to a related problem, with wing slot assemblies. The 'stall control strips' had originally been installed under T.O. 01-60-05 circa December 4, 1940, but this entire matter was in fact a reinstallation as Wright Field engineering claimed that the stall control strips gave better results than the slots, many of which had been wired shut by mechanics on the field.

At least eight BT-9s were lost in crashes attributed to the poor stall characteristics. One (AC36-42) survived in service into August 1945. The first BT-9 (S/N AC36-28) was delivered August 10, 1935, and assigned to Chanute Field, although most BT-9s ended up at one time or another at Randolph Field in Texas. The per unit cost was $14,111.71.

Astute readers will note that Mfg. S/N NA-19-2 seems to be missing from this entire range of numbers (S/N NA-19-4 was a BT-9A). Apparently, this airframe became Mfg. S/N NA-16-2, as it is otherwise unaccounted for.

NA-19A (BT-9A)

NAA Designation:	NA-19A
NAA Charge Number:	NA-19A
Mfg. S/N:	NA-19-4, 12 to 19, 35 to 49, 68 to 83
User Regn. or S/N:	ACR36-88 to 36-127

A total of 40 BT-9As were also ordered on the same contract as the BT-9s, Contract AC-7881. Interestingly, these were originally cited in Air Corps correspondence and documents as "BT-9 (Organized Reserve)." The first example, AC36-88, was accepted by the AC on the same day as the first BT-9, August 10, 1935. The unit cost was $13,481.21, less than the BT-9s. This first aircraft was assigned to Bolling Field. Others, in keeping with the avowed purpose of assignment to the Air Corps Reserve, were scattered in small numbers at Reserve bases, such as Memphis, Boston and Salt Lake City.

The differences between the BT-9 and BT-9A offer spotters and collectors some interesting recognition features. Although externally they were visually similar, the BT-9A could be equipped with a Type K-3B Camera, Type RC-16 Interphone set and more importantly,

A rather primitive Air Corps three-view silhouette shows the general planform of the BT-9 (NA-19), BT-9B and BT-9C. The series featured a tall radio mast, offset to the right side of the forward fuselage, and a prominent exhaust stack coming out of the lower right side of the cowling. (USAF)

This BT-9 bears Randolph's 46th School Squadron number 276 in late 1941. The lower portion of the wheel spats were frequently removed while in service on virtually every version so equipped to avoid debris accumulation. (Fred Bamberger Collection via Peter M. Bowers)

The chronic and abrupt stall characteristics of the BT-9s led Wright Field to attempt a number of possible fixes, including this unusual wing-tip installation, as seen at Lambert Field, St. Louis, Missouri. (USAF via National Archives, RG 18)

had provisions for a .30-caliber Browning M-1 fixed machine gun over the starboard (right) side of the nose (configured for 200 rounds of ammunition) and a similar weapon on a flexible mounting in the rear cockpit (500 rounds of ammunition). The Radio Compass and Marker Beacon found in the BT-9 were eliminated in the BT-9A, as were the flight instruments from the observer's cockpit. Minor changes were also made in the BT-9A's controls, rear cockpit, baggage compartment, seats and rear hood to provide for the installation of the photographic equipment (sometimes erroneously cited as a "camera gun") and armament.

These aircraft were intentionally purchased specifically for issue to the Organized Reserve (as it was known at the time), and were clearly more operational than Basic Trainer aircraft. The earliest known USAAC Aircraft Branch Inspection Report for a BT-9A is dated September 1, 1936 and cited the designation as "BT-9 (Organized Reserve)." The wing tip stall problem of the BT-9 was allegedly "solved" on the BT-9A by building a 2-degree "wash-out" into the outer wing panels. The BT-9As were also lengthened by a total of five inches to improve its overall stability.

The BT-9A (NA-19A) was the first U.S. service version of the NA-16 family to be armament capable. This example, USAAC S/N 36-121, also shows the additional intake and vent just aft of the cowling and the shorter, broader radio mast of the BT-9A. The 40 BT-9As were purchased for the Air Corps Organized Reserve. This aircraft spent its entire service life at Brooks, Stinson, Chanute and Shepard fields before it was surveyed due to wear and tear on June 30, 1943. (via Bob Esposito)

16 WARBIRDTECH SERIES

The last BT-9A on the USAAF books (S/N 36-97) was finally dropped from the books in January 1945.

NA-20

NAA Designation:	NA-16-2H
NAA Charge Number:	NA-20
Mfg. S/N:	NA-16-2
User Regn. or S/N:	X-16025, NC-16025, NR16025, Honduran Air Force S/N 20

NAA records describe this aircraft as "similar to the BT-9—for demonstration in China." Unusually, no contract date was given with the Charge Number, suggesting that this aircraft was intended as a demonstration aircraft from the start. Fitted with an unknown variant of the Whirlwind engine and an unknown combination of armament installations, this demonstrator is credited with winning a Chinese Nationalist Government order for 35 NA-41s.

Upon its return to the United States after its Chinese demonstration tour, the NA-20 was fitted with a 550HP Pratt & Whitney Wasp (S/N 6159), then exported to the Honduran Air Force, at which point it was given S/N 20. The aircraft was flight-delivered to Tegucigalpa by Harold White and another U.S. pilot, arriving on March 4, 1938. Incredible as it may seem, I saw the hulk of this aircraft at Tegucigalpa as late as 1979, and if it is still there, it is certainly the oldest surviving NA-16 variant in the world.

During its Honduran service, the aircraft carried two .30-caliber weapons—one over the starboard nose cowling, synchronized, and one in the rear cockpit, flexible—plus bomb racks under the center section of the fuselage.

This close-up view shows the lower rear fuselage and tail wheel of a BT-9, November 15, 1936. (USAF 57294AC via National Archives, Sarah Clark Collection)

The solitary NA-16-2H (NA-20) after its return from China, curiously bears U.S. commercial registration number NC-16025, for which it was not eligible, since it did not receive an Approved Type Certificate (ATC) from the CAA. It had properly carried Restricted License NR-16025 during its demonstration sojourn to China. In this view, the nose gun installation that it featured when it was finally exported to Honduras in 1937 is not evident. (NAA 20.101/166 via David W. Ostrowski)

NA-22

NAA Designation:	NA-22
NAA Charge Number:	NA-22
Mfg. S/N:	NA-19-11*
User Regn. or S/N:	(AC 36-36)

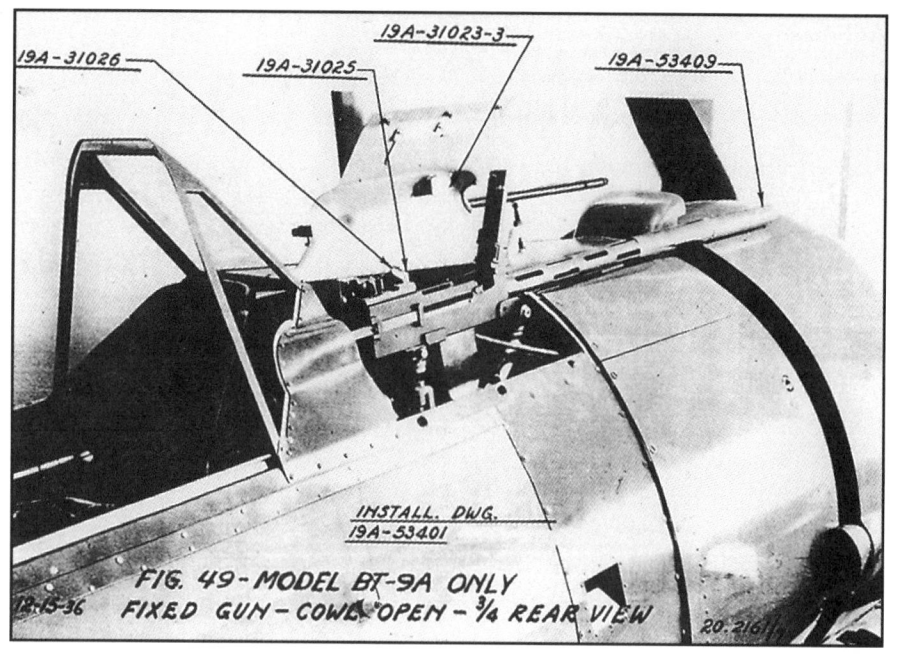

Shown are the details of the starboard, fixed Browning M-1 .30-caliber gun sight and blast tube on a BT-9A and the new, rather reduced exhaust on the lower rear side of the cowling, as it appeared in mid-December 1936. (Air Corps T.O. 01-60C-2)

The single NA-22 is usually cited as having been nothing more than the ninth production BT-9. It was re-engined with a 225HP Wright R-760ET (J-6-7) Whirlwind (S/N 14317), given open cockpits similar to the original NA-16, and entered in the "Air Corps Circular Proposal No. 36-28 (PT Demonstration)," allegedly with the consent of the Air Corps. The aircraft supposedly was flown with and without the speed ring cowl shown, but it was found to be underpowered for its weight.

The official Wright Field performance test for this unusual aircraft was dated July 7, 1936. Most sources state that the NA-22 was eventually reconfigured as a standard BT-9, then later returned to the Air Corps. However, the Individual Aircraft Record Card for S/N 36-36 does not bear any evidence of this, which opens up questions of the origins of previously published information and the correct origins of this aircraft.

NA-23 (BT-9B)

NAA Designation:	NA-23
NAA Charge Number:	NA-23
Mfg. S/N:	NA-23-85 to NA-23-201
User Regn. or S/N:	AC37-115 to 37-231

Ordered on Contract AC-9345, which was dated December 1, 1936, these 117 BT-9Bs incorporated minor changes that were learned from the fielding of its BT-9 and BT-9A predecessors. The BT-9Bs had no armament provisions whatsoever. The first example was turned over to the USAAC on November 18, 1936, at a unit cost of $14,630.43, and it was assigned (as were most of the others) to Randolph Field, Texas. BT-9Bs were the first Air Corps NA-16 variants to be assigned overseas, when S/N 37-190, -191, -192 and -193 were

The rather spartan but functional rear cockpit instrument panel of a BT-9A could mount a flexible rear gun, as well as a K-3B camera below the rear seat area. (Air Corps T.O. 01-60C-2)

18

• SPIN RECOVERY MODIFICATIONS •

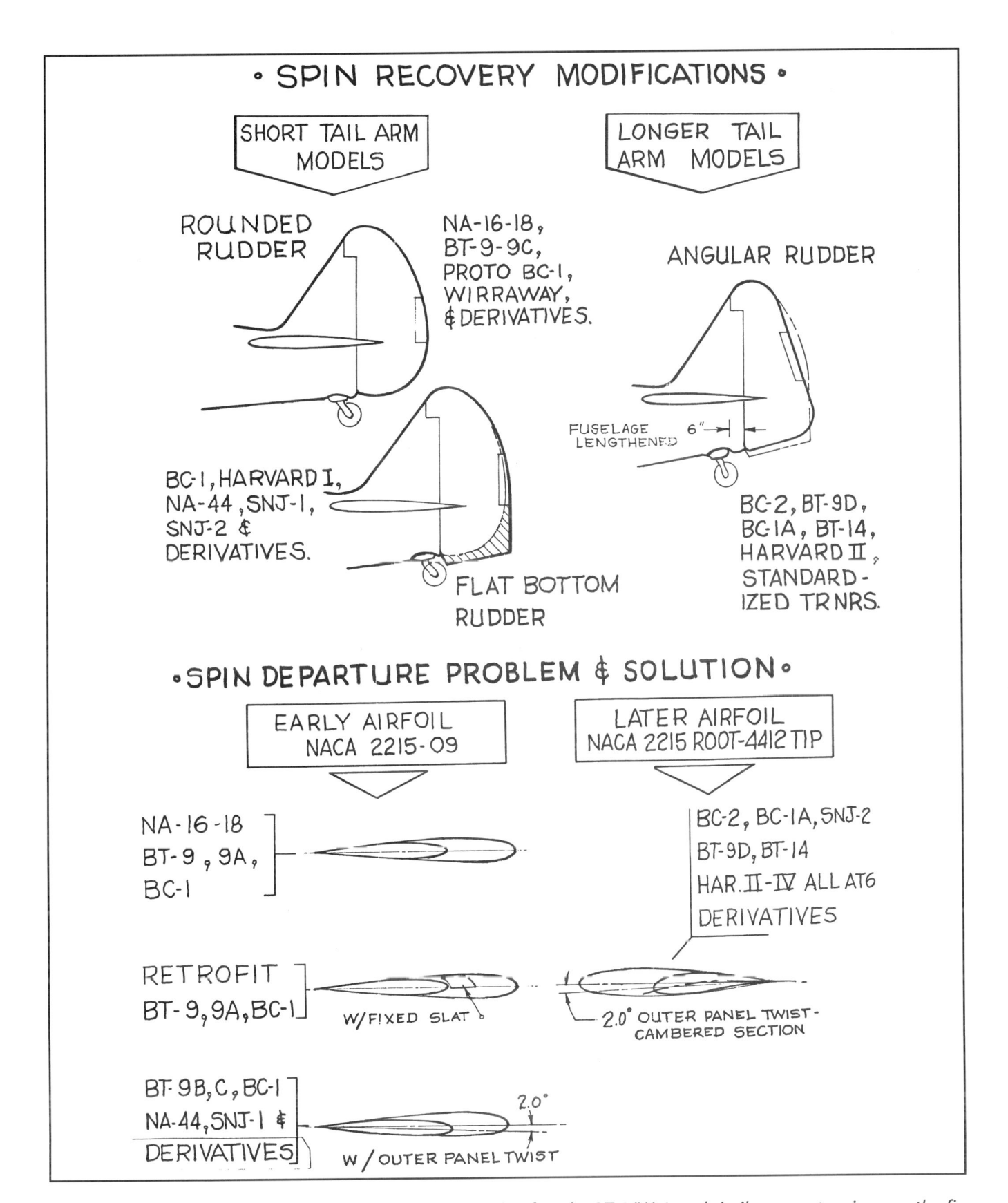

SHORT TAIL ARM MODELS

ROUNDED RUDDER

NA-16-18, BT-9-9C, PROTO BC-1, WIRRAWAY, & DERIVATIVES.

BC-1, HARVARD I, NA-44, SNJ-1, SNJ-2 & DERIVATIVES.

FLAT BOTTOM RUDDER

LONGER TAIL ARM MODELS

ANGULAR RUDDER

FUSELAGE LENGTHENED 6"

BC-2, BT-9D, BC-1A, BT-14, HARVARD II, STANDARDIZED TRNRS.

• SPIN DEPARTURE PROBLEM & SOLUTION •

EARLY AIRFOIL NACA 2215-09

NA-16-18, BT-9, 9A, BC-1

RETROFIT BT-9, 9A, BC-1 — W/FIXED SLAT

LATER AIRFOIL NACA 2215 ROOT-4412 TIP

BC-2, BC-1A, SNJ-2, BT-9D, BT-14, HAR. II-IV ALL AT6 DERIVATIVES

2.0° OUTER PANEL TWIST - CAMBERED SECTION

BT-9B, C, BC-1, NA-44, SNJ-1 & DERIVATIVES — W/OUTER PANEL TWIST 2.0°

The true secret to the ultimate success of the AT-6 family after the BT-9/NJ-1 and similar export series was the fix that dealt with the vicious stall characteristics of the early variants. This series of drawings shows the evolution of the rudder changes, wing warping or twisting and the ultimate six-inch lengthening of the vertical tail area that was the final solution. (Courtesy of Frank Compton)

split between Hickam and Wheeler fields in Hawaii on November 6, 1937. They returned to Randolph Field in January 1940.

One aircraft, S/N 37-208, was converted to become the solitary **BT-9D** on October 7, 1937, and was assigned to Chanute Field. It was finally surplused in December 1944.

NA-26 (BC-1)

NAA Designation:	(BC-1)
NAA Charge Number:	NA-26
Mfg. S/N:	26-202
User Regn. or S/N:	X-18990, N-18990

The NA-26 has really never received due credit for its place in the evolution of the Texan family, and in the bargain, it is something of a mystery aircraft. It had been described, initially as "the demonstrator for the Basic Combat Trainer" per USAAC Circular Proposal No.37-220, and as, "similar to the BT-9 but with a larger engine, armament, retractable landing gear, and powered by a Pratt & Whitney R-1304-40 Wasp." In truth, this aircraft was the precursor of all of the retractable gear

Incredibly, the same aircraft, the solitary NA-16-2H (NA-20) standing derelict at Tegucigalpa, Honduras, in September 1980, bearing a Honduran Air Force logo on the fuselage. (Carlos Planas)

The solitary NA-22 was North American's entry in a July 1936 Air Corps Primary Trainer competition, which it did not win. Although it is frequently cited (apparently without foundation) as a "borrowed" Air Corps BT-9 (S/N 36-36) fitted with a 235HP Wright R-760ET Whirlwind, the records do not support this contention. The aircraft was tested first without a speed ring (May 1936), then at Wright Field in July with such an installation, and it was found to be underpowered for its weight. (NAA 20.101/168 via Fred Freeman)

The short-lived NA-22 as tested at Wright Field in July 1936 with a speed ring. It is not clear how this aircraft was allowed to fly, as it was apparently not Air Corps property (the official test report stated "Air Corps No.: None," in spite of previous reports to the contrary and the insignia painted on) and no U.S. experimental license number is known for it. (Wright Field No.54466, National Archives, Sarah Clark Collection)

20 WARBIRDTECH SERIES

BT-9B (NA-23), Air Corps S/N 37-227, shows yet another experiment to fix the unpleasant stall characteristics of the BT-9 series, at Langley Field, Virginia, in May 1939. It had gone on loan to NACA from Wright Field November 21, 1938, and did not return from there until May 12, 1941. It survived Wright Field to be surplused at McKellar Field in September 1944. (USAF G-1058-1-852L-1AB, National Archives RG18)

USAAC variants that followed. The BC-1 is often described rather inelegantly as "an NJ-1 with retractable landing gear," but it is one that retained the fabric fuselage covering. Peter M. Bowers described this aircraft as "essentially the NA-18 with retractable landing gear, a foot more wing span and seven square feet more wing area." The NA-26 also had provision for two .30-caliber guns, including the standard flexible gun, and for the first time, either the standard nose-mounted synchronized unit or a gun mounted in the inner right wing panel.

The NA-26 was apparently tested extensively at Wright Field in full period USAAC colors and markings, although it was every inch a company-owned aircraft. It also flew sans the U.S. civil Identification Mark that it was supposed to have been wearing—Initially X-18990 and later Identified Aircraft Mark N-18990.

The fifth BT-9B, Air Corps S/N 37-119, bearing Randolph Field number 231, shows details of the tall radio mast, rear-view mirror and distinctive cowling vents in October 1937. (USAF 14133AC, National Archives RG18)

Close-up view of the canopy frames an Air Corps data block on BT-9B S/N 37-119 at Randolph Field in October 1937 when it was just five months old. It served its entire life at Randolph, and it was wrecked west of Davenport Auxiliary Field, Texas on December 29, 1940. (USAF 14134AC, National Archives RG18).

NORTH AMERICAN
NA-16/AT-6/SNJ

Instrument panel of BT-9B USAAC S/N 37-218 circa August 1938. Compare this with the basic BT-9 shown earlier. It had been originally accepted November 17, 1937, and assigned to the Reserve unit at Hamilton Field, but it went to Randolph Field in March 1939, where it served out its days until it was wrecked near Bryan, Texas, on July 21, 1943. (USAF G456-467J-PD, National Archives, RG18)

One of the most significant, and least heralded, aircraft in the entire NA-16 family, was the solitary NA-26. Entered in the Air Corps design competition for the new Basic Combat series at Wright Field in March 1937, it was the first to actually feature retractable landing gear and it defined the basic AT-6 look for years to come. Despite the Air Corps insignia, it was actually a civil aircraft and was supposed to bear Experimental marks X-18990. It was sold to Canada July 23, 1940, where it ended its days in obscurity. (NAA 20.101/201 via David W. Ostrowski)

This aircraft was sold to Canada July 23, 1940, on Contract CAN-40 and became RCAF S/N 3345. Interestingly, the Canadians state on RCAF records that "it was converted to Harvard II standard," a fact not previously published. The NA-26 was finally stricken as Category A on May 20, 1942. As historian Colonel John deVries put it, this "evolution of the retracting main landing gear and the 550/600HP Wasp S3H1 engine took the design out of the fundamental or basic flight training category and thrust it into a far greater instructional tool than ever anticipated."

NA-27

NAA DESIGNATION:	NA-16-2H
NAA CHARGE NUMBER:	NA-27
MFG. S/N:	27-312
USER REGN. OR S/N:	R-17377, PH-APG, RNAAF 997

Often described in NAA and other publications as a "Basic Combat Trainer for European demonstrations and similar to the NA-26," the single NA-27 built was another rather strangely fated aircraft. The date of the NAA Charge Number (with Fokker in the Netherlands listed as the "customer") is December 1, 1936 (the same date as the first BT-9B). However, photos of the aircraft bearing Restricted Identification Number R-17377 are dated as late as April 15, 1937, and in these photos, the aircraft clearly has fixed main gear and armament provisions.

The fate of this aircraft is now clear for the first time. Indeed sold to Fokker, it gained Dutch civil registration PH-APG on July 21, 1937, and appears in later period photos in full Royal Netherlands Army Air Force markings (camouflaged with

The solitary NA-27 "European Demonstrator" bears U.S. Restricted marks R-17377 in mid-April 1937. It was sold to Fokker. (NAA 20.101/183 via David W. Ostrowski)

orange "triangle" national insignia) with their serial number 997. The aircraft had been impressed by the Dutch Army on September 1, 1939, and was assigned to the Advanced Flight School at the island of Texel. It was lost to German Bf 110 fighter-bombers on May 11, 1940.

NA-28 (NJ-1)

NAA Designation:	(NJ-1)
NAA Charge Number:	NA-28
Mfg. S/N:	28 313
User Regn. or S/N:	Bu. No. 0910 to 0949

Procured for the U.S. Navy via a USAAC Contract (AC-9345, dated December 14, 1936, Navy Requisition No. 327-37), these 40 NJ-1s were the first North American Aviation aircraft procured by the Navy. Although usually described as "BT-9s modified for the USN," the Navy described the aircraft this way: "The NJ-1 airplane is a single engine, two seat, taper wing monoplane designed for advanced training. The wheels are fixed, but a dummy retractable landing gear control operates landing indicators. It is not equipped for gunnery, bombing or carrier operations. The power plant is a Pratt & Whitney R-1340-6 of 550hp."

The "European Demonstrator" NA-27 wears Dutch civil registration PH-APG. It later passed into the Royal Netherlands Army Air Force before the German invasion in May 1940. (Fokker)

The new and the old. A U.S. Navy NJ-1 (NA-28) poses in front of a brace of elderly Vought Corsairs in this November 1937 Pensacola Naval Air Station view. The pre-WW2 Navy training colors were memorable, with red bands on the wings and fuselage, cowling and empennage, while serving as instrument trainers. They had no armament capability. (USN PNX-15411, National Archives)

NORTH AMERICAN NA-16/AT-6/SNJ

U.S. Navy NJ-1 Bu. No.0922 is in flight in late January 1938, complete with a swab in the rear seat near Pensacola, Florida. This aircraft had been delivered December 31, 1937, and it was finally stricken at Olathe on November 25, 1944. (USN PNX-15565, National Archives)

Complete with the two-star placard of a Navy flag officer and special color scheme, a few NJ-1s saw service as "Admiral's Barge" aircraft. (via Peter M. Bowers)

Accelerated service tests for the NJ-1 were carried out at Pensacola Naval Air Station (NAS) by VN5D8 until January 3, 1938. The first aircraft, Bu. No. 0910, had been accepted and delivered there on July 3, 1937, serving until August 1943. The testing unit concluded that the NJ-1 was "suitable for use as an advanced training plane," but noted not fewer than 45 discrepancies, ranging from minor recommendations dealing with the "rather thin canopy cockpit tracks," which should have "a prominent no-step sign painted under them," to the far more serious observation that "the stall characteristics under all conditions are extremely abrupt, with a tendency to violently whip onto its back when stalled, with little tendency for the nose to drop." The unit also noted, "the stall characteristics for take-off with the flaps down are poor."

The author of the report, when expounding on the stall characteristics included the somewhat humorous statement: "There is a positive feeling that the stick is being held hard over to the side by the occupant of the other cockpit" when attempting corrective control movements. Another interesting observation noted, "the fuselage, and it is thought, particularly the bracing behind the pilot's head has become magnetized, causing large compass errors, in one case as large as 45 degrees." With regard to the

Late in its service life, Navy NJ-1 Bu. No.0947 was by July 1943 doped aluminum overall in this Anacostia NAS view. Originally accepted January 19, 1938, it served in turn at Anacostia, Norfolk, Pensacola and NRAB Memphis before it was stricken on January 31, 1943. (via Peter M. Bowers)

stall characteristics the report said, "it is not recommended that this plane be used to train students for night flying," which was a decided drawback in an advanced trainer, and "sometimes the aircraft stalls to the right and sometimes to the left, with varying degrees of speed on the fall off." It was also observed that the plastic canopy failed "in several places at the after-end in the corners" during the tests.

According to one source, the 40th and last NJ-1 (Bu. No. 0949) was tested by NAA and the Navy with a 550HP Ranger XV-770-4, receiving the temporary designation of NJ-2. The experiment was reportedly a failure, and the aircraft reverted to standard NJ 1 configuration. However, I could find not a shred of evidence to support this contention. The Individual Aircraft Record Card for Bu. No. 0949 reflects no such change, although it did show an engine change from the original R-1340-7 to an R-1340-18 in March 1940. The aircraft survived until it was stricken on July 31, 1944, at NAS Bunker Hill, Indiana.

This is a rare look at the "front office" of a U.S. Navy NJ-1 as it appeared in January 1938. (USN PNX-15567, National Archives)

NA-29 (BT-9C)

NAA Designation: (BT-9C)
NAA Charge Number: NA-29
Mfg. S/N: 29-353 to 29-385; 29-505 to 29-538
User Regn. or S/N: ACR37-383 to 37-415 and ACR38-224 to 38-257

A total of 67 BT-9Cs were procured under a single contract (AC-9345) dated December 22, 1936, all intended for the Air Corps Reserves. The second batch of 34 aircraft ordered was an increase on Contract Charge No. 10. While these aircraft were assigned Basic Trainer series designations, the BT-9Cs had the character of light tactical aircraft, just like the earlier and similar BT-9As.

The first example, S/N 37-38, was delivered November 18, 1936, to

A dedicated instrument trainer, the rear cockpit instrument panel of a Navy NJ-1 was far more complete that a comparable Army BT-9. The "Landing Gear Warning" placard is for training only; the NJ-1s had fixed gear. (USN PNX-15569, National Archives)

Coded "6/9ƟR," this BT-9C (NA-29) was photographed at Oakland, California, in October 1940. This aircraft was probably assigned to the 9th Corps Reserve element. The numeral that appears to be an "8" is actually an "O" for observation, intersected by a horizontal bar. Like the earlier BT-9As, the BT-9Cs were capable of bearing armament (fixed and flexible) and had space for a T-3A camera, but it had no radio compass or marker beacons and no flight instruments in the rear cockpit. Many were assigned to Reserve commands. (Peter M. Bowers)

A cadet sweats it out "under the hood" in BT-9C, S/N 38-227 (Randolph Field No. 496), in August 1940. The upper deck gun mounting is just visible, as is the trough cover for the rear gun when mounted. This aircraft was accepted June 17, 1938, and was initially assigned to a Reserve unit at Chicago, later moving to Randolph Field (53rd School Squadron), where it served out its time. It was surveyed at Goodfellow Field on June 25, 1943. (USAF 33485AC, National Archives RG18)

One BT-9B was converted to become the solitary BT-9D, USAAC S/N 37-208, receiving a BC-1A type wing and tail surfaces and a Wright R-975-7 engine. It was assigned to Chanute Field, served out its life there and was surplused in December 1944. (USAF 19493AC, National Archives RG18)

Wright Field, but it later went to an Air Corps Reserve unit at Columbus, Ohio. Others were assigned to ACR units at Long Beach, Chicago and other major cities, but most survivors eventually ended up at Randolph Field, Texas. The unit cost for a BT-9C was $14,630.93. The first aircraft, S/N 37-383, was completed as the solitary Y1BT-10.

The BT-9C retained the R-975-7 engine with a few minor improvements, such as canvas covered walkways on the center section on each side of the fuselage and new steps installed on the left side of the fuselage to ease entry and egress—a key recognition feature. The BT-9Cs were provisioned for .30-caliber fixed and flexible guns, Type BC-16 interphones and a Type T-3A camera. The radio compass and marker beacons were eliminated, as were the flight instruments from what was termed the observer's cockpit.

Temporary fixed-wing slats on the outboard leading edges of each wing tamed the poor stall characteristics, as noted earlier. However, with their rather narrow landing gear track, the entire BT-9 series was also notoriously top heavy, and this feature, coupled with unpredictable braking habits, accounted for a considerable number of accidents.

Although the first aircraft in this series, S/N 37-383, has always been cited as the "first BT-9C," its Individual Aircraft History Card does not reflect this. The only designation ever recorded on the card was Y1BT-10.

There was also a single BT-9D. According to some sources, this was a BT-9B that had been rebuilt with new wing panels (similar to the BC-1A) and tail surfaces, possibly as a fix for the unfortunate stall characteristics of earlier variants. Other sources claim it was the elusive NA-26. In truth, this aircraft was built as a BT-9B. If there is a resemblance to the BT-14, it is not coincidental. The changes made to create the BT-9D justified the production of the BT-14.

The solitary Y1BT-10 (NA-29) was the first BT-9C re-engined with a 600HP Pratt & Whitney R-1340-41 in 1938, retaining most other characteristics including, in this Wright Field view, a gun sight. Note the absence of leading edge slats. (USAF 13574AC, National Archives RG18)

The single Y1BT-10, now redesignated as simply BT-10, bears the insignia of an unidentified Air Corps Reserve unit on mid-fuselage. At this point, the gun sight noted in the earlier illustration had been deleted and leading-edge slats were in place. Note the retainer on the upper rear fuselage decking for the flexible gun when stowed. (William T. Larkins via David W. Ostrowski)

Frequently illustrated, the single Royal Swedish Air Force NA-16-4M (NA-31) was the sole example of the Sk 14 (Swedish designation) to bear this unique presentation of the Swedish national insignia: black crowns on a white disc and a blue and gold rudder. The fuselage was a slate gray color while the wings and horizontal tail surfaces were a shade of orange. The RSwAF serial was 671; the digit "5" indicating F5 (Training) Wing, and "55" the number within unit. (NAA 20.101/190 via David W. Ostrowski)

NORTH AMERICAN
NA-16/AT-6/SNJ

The single NA-16-1A (NA-32), similar in many respects to the U.S. Navy NJ-1 and Army Air Corps Y1BT-10, was sold to the Royal Australian Air Force, where it became A20-1 on February 2, 1938, and was one of the two aircraft that gave impetus to the Australian derivative, the Wirraway (aboriginal for "Challenge"). (NAA 20.101/193 via David W. Ostrowski)

Along with the NA-32, Australia also imported the single NA-16-2K (NA-33), and following evaluation, this was the aircraft that served as the basis for the Wirraway. With a retractable landing gear, three-bladed prop and enhanced armament capability, it seemed ideal for Australian requirements of 1938. (NAA 20.201/115 via David W. Ostrowski)

NA-29 and NA-30 (Y1BT-10)

NAA Designation:	(Y1BT-10)
NAA Charge Number:	NA-29 and NA-30
Mfg. S/N:	29-385
User Regn. or S/N:	ACR37-383

The single Y1BT-10 was actually ordered originally in the BT-9C's first production run and has often been cited as S/N 37-383. However, it was completed as the Y1BT-10 and engined with a 600HP R-1340-41. It was delivered as such to Wright Field on November 18, 1936, before it moved to Bolling Field in Washington, DC. The Y1BT-10 was redesignated the BT-10 just prior to its assignment to Mines Field in California during November 1941, and ended its days at the University of California at Santa Barbara via the Reconstruction Finance Corporation in October 1943.

The circumstances leading to this one-off are rather confusing. One source states that the aircraft was developed to a Navy requirement, born out of the fact that the Navy did not make use of the Wright R-975 engine series, preferring the Pratt & Whitney series instead. As the story goes, NAA installed the R-1340-41, creating the Y1BT-10, and from this emerged the Navy's NJ-1, the first of the NAA series built to use the Pratt & Whitney engine.

The first Wirraway Mark I built under license, based on the NA-33, flew on March 8, 1939, and the first production examples followed in July. NAA made a bundle on the Australian license rights. The aircraft pictured is a CA 7 Wirraway II variant, RAAF serial A20-202. Note the 'bead' sight on the forward fuselage between the .303-caliber guns. (CAC)

28 WARBIRDTECH SERIES

The Argentine Army Aviation Command acquired, along with the very first NA-18, 30 NA-16-1P (NA-34s) commencing in March 1938. Note the two forward-firing 7.7MM guns over the nose, and the radio mast square in the middle, between them. The NA-34s were considered tactical aircraft. Interestingly, mainly due to the success of the NA-34s (and the indigenous I.Ae. 22), the Argentine Air Force was the only Latin American air arm not to acquire AT-6s post-war. Some survived into 1955. (NAA 20.201/164 via David W. Ostrowski)

While there may be some truth to this extraordinary display of inter-service cooperation during lean budgetary times, the USAAC Aircraft Branch at Wright Field conducted a thorough Inspection Report on the Y1BT-10 that was dated June 7, 1937. The Air Corps went so far as to suggest to NAA that, if funding could be found, production (as the NA-30/BT-10) might be forthcoming. Apparently, though, the promise of the BC-1 transcended this, and the NA-30 remained a "Drawings Only" paper project.

NA-31

NAA DESIGNATION:	NA-16-4M
NAA CHARGE NUMBER:	NA-31
MFG. S/N:	31-386
USER REGN. OR S/N:	RSwAF 671 coded 5+55

Similar visually to the BT-9C but with a different engine and

Silhouette of the BC-1 (NA-36), the first production USAAC NA-16 descendent to feature retractable landing gear as standard. The RDF loop under the forward fuselage, amidship radio mast and square rudder base were key recognition features. (USAAC)

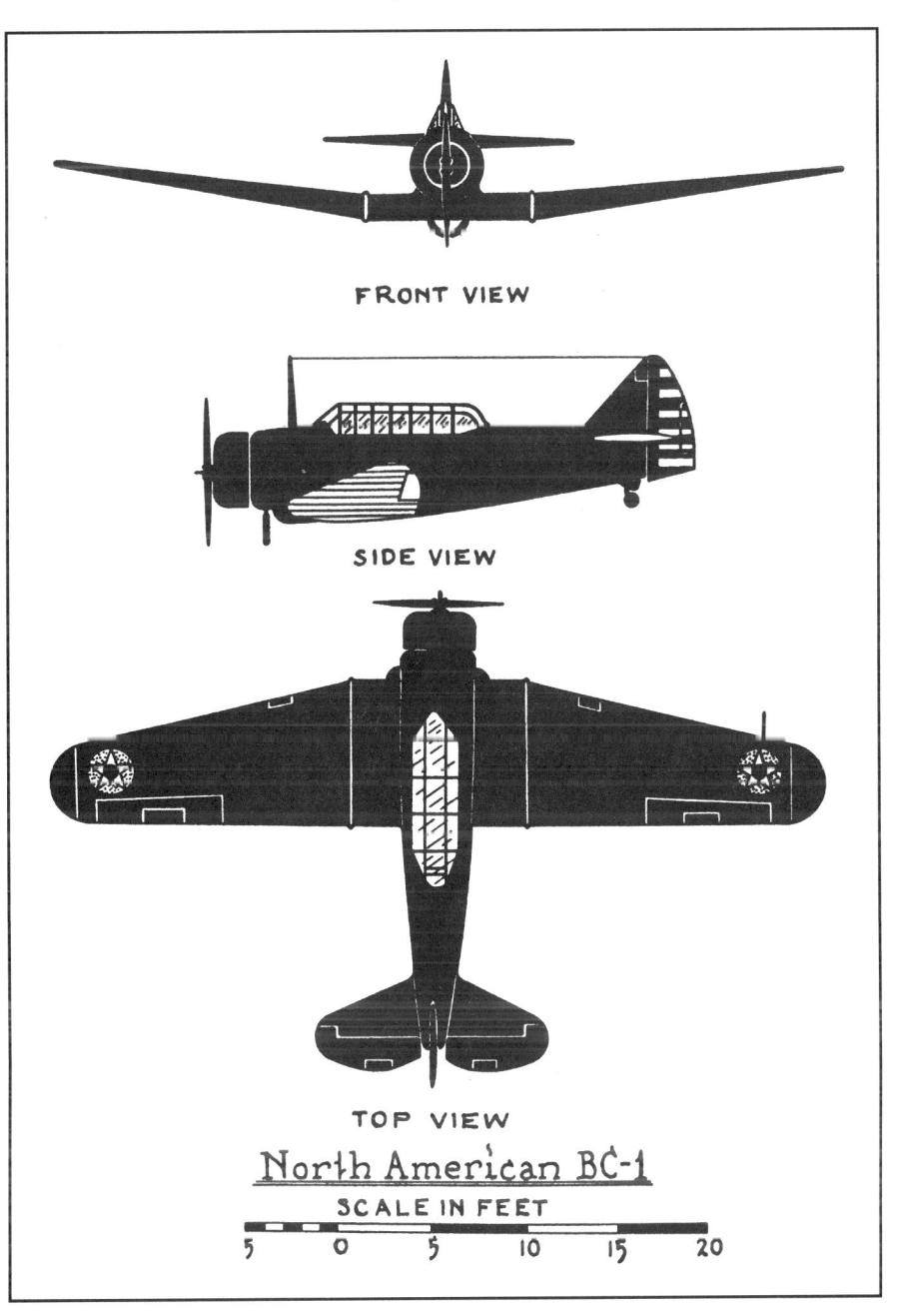

NORTH AMERICAN
NA-16/AT-6/SNJ

29

At least four Swedish NA-16-4M derivatives were modified with this unique tri-cycle undercarriage arrangement as part of tests for the SAAB J 21A indigenous fighter program. (SAAB via Peter Liander)

Goodyear Airwheels, NAA General Order (a change of terms from the more often used Charge Number) NA-31 was dated February 8, 1937. This order called for one complete aircraft, probably to serve as a pattern, and a license to build the type in Sweden by AB Svenska Jarnvagsverkstaderna (ASJA), and later by SAAB. NAA termed this contract completed on November 15, 1937, which was probably the delivery date of the NA-16-4M to Sweden.

Subsequently, a total of 53 of these aircraft were built with Swedish license-built 455HP Wright R-975-E3 engines, under RSwAF serials 603 to 609, 672 to 699 and 5810 to 5827. They were built by ASJA for the Royal Swedish Air Force (Flygvapnet) using their designation of Sk 14. The first of the Swedish-built machines entered service in May 1939. ASJA built 23 more aircraft as the Sk 14A (S/N 5828 to 5850) with the 525HP Piaggio P VIIc RC35 radial engine. Then SAAB built 60 more Sk 14s to fill a 1942 order. These were unusual due to their fixed-pitch wooden props, and in many cases, the distinctive landing gear fairing was removed to accommodate Sweden's rather harsh field operating conditions. The RSwAF later acquired many other surplus AT-6s and AT-16s from war surplus stocks.

One Sk 14 aircraft, 5+105, underwent a unique transformation by SAAB when it was fitted with a tri-cycle undercarriage to test the geometry and characteristics of the indigenous SAAB 21A fighter.

NA-32

NAA Designation:	NA-16-1A
NAA Charge Number:	NA-32
Mfg. S/N:	32-387
User Regn. or S/N:	RAAF A20-1

Another milestone NAA export order was the single NA-32 aircraft, which was built under General Order NA-32 for the Australian Government. Also sold were the accompanying license rights to build the type by the Commonwealth Aircraft Corporation, dated March 10, 1937.

The NA-32 was very similar to the U.S. Navy's NJ-1 and the Y1BT-10 discussed earlier. This aircraft was incorporated into the Royal Australian Air Force and given their serial number A20-1, which was a dual-purpose serial indicating the RAAF type (A20-) and the fact that it was the number one aircraft of that type (-1). The Australians opted not to exercise their manufacturing rights for the NA-32, electing instead to go with the NA-33, which they had acquired at the same time.

NA-33

NAA Designation:	NA-16-2K
NAA Charge Number:	NA-33
Mfg. S/N:	33-388
User Regn. or S/N:	RAAF A20-2

Facing Nordic weather conditions, the Royal Swedish Air Force developed skis for installation on both the NA-16-4M (Sk 14) they acquired, as well as later Harvard IIbs and other Texan variants. (Bror Andrrssen via Peter Liander)

The Australian Government, at the recommendation of Wing Commander Lawrence J. Wackett, had placed orders with NAA for single examples of the NA-32 and NA-33, with manufacturing rights for both types. This followed a tour of aircraft manufacturing firms in Europe and the United States, including North American. Wackett sought a design that could be manufactured in conjunction with Australia's defense effort that contained no "bugs"—i.e., something a brand-new industry could build, as well as something that would stand the wear of the race of design.

Wackett acquired not only the rights for the NA-32 and NA-33, but the Pratt & Whitney engines that were to power them—the R-1340-S1H1G 600HP variant, most but not all of which, were also built by CAC. Australian production tooling commenced on the CA-1 Wirraway I (40 were built) in April 1938. The first Australian-built example did not fly until March 27, 1939. These CA-1s were followed by 60 CA-3s, 32 CA-5s, 100 CA-7s, 200 CA-8s and 188 CA-9s, which were all collectively identified in service as Wirraway IIs, and 135 CA-16 Wirraway IIIs. A total of 755 aircraft were built, although some orders were apparently canceled, as a total of 811 had been ordered. All were built at CAC's Fishermen's Bend factory near Melbourne. What is not generally known, is that 233 of these hybrid aircraft were funded by Great Britain under the Empire Air Training Scheme.

PILOT'S CHECK LIST

BC-1, BC-1A, AT-6, AT-6A, AT-6B, AT-6C, AT-6D,
SNJ-3, SNJ-4, SNJ-5 Airplanes
R-1340-47, R-1340-49, R-1340-AN-1 Engines

BEFORE STARTING ENGINE
1. Check Form 1 (Navy Yellow Sheet).
2. Check Form F—Weight and Balance Clearance (AN-01-1-40).
3. Set parking brakes.
4. UNLOCK surface controls and check for freedom of operation.
5. Fuel selector—Reserve—check for quantity.
6. Propeller HIGH PITCH.
7. Mixture FULL RICH.
8. Throttle 600-800 RPM.
9. Carburetor Heat COLD.
10. Prime 4 to 6 strokes when cold.
11. Generator main line switches ON.
12. Battery switch ON (Not applicable to BC-1).
13. Ignition switch BOTH ON.
14. Energize and engage starter.

DURING WARM-UP
1. Oil pressure up, shift propeller to LOW PITCH.
2. Warm up at 1000 RPM.
3. Check magnetos at 1800 RPM. Max. drop 100 RPM.
4. Check operation of: propeller control, flaps, elevator and rudder trim, and generator.
5. Check radio, clock and altimeter.

BEFORE TAKE-OFF
1. Propeller INCREASE RPM (low pitch).
2. Mixture RICH.
3. Carburetor heat COLD.
4. Oil temperature 40°C minimum, 95°C maximum.
5. Cylinder temperature 25°C minimum, 260°C maximum.
6. Take off 36 in. Hg 2250 RPM.

DURING FLIGHT
1. Landing gear UP.
2. Flaps UP.
3. Maximum diving RPM 2640.
4. Maximum diving speed 240 IAS.
5. Do not intentionally spin more than one turn.

6. **ALLOWABLE ENGINE OPERATION**
   Climb and High Speed (Normal Rated Power).
   RPM 2200
   Manifold pressure 32.5 in. Hg.
   Mixture Control FULL RICH.
   AT-6 Series
   Maximum Cruising
   RPM 1925
   Manifold Pressure 29.0 in. Hg.
   Mixture Control SMOOTH OPERATION TO BEST POWER.
   Desired Cruising
   RPM 1850
   Manifold pressure 26.0 in. Hg.
   Mixture Control SMOOTH OPERATION TO BEST POWER.
   Cruise For Minimum Specific Fuel Flow
   RPM 1700
   Manifold pressure 26.0 in. Hg.
   Mixture Control BEST POWER.

BEFORE LANDING
1. Landing gear DOWN.
2. The Emergency Lock position will not be used in normal operation of the Landing Gear.
3. Propeller 1925 RPM.
4. Mixture RICH.
5. Fuel selector on RESERVE.
6. Flaps as required (Do not lower above 126 IAS.)
7. CAGE turn and flight indicators.

AFTER LANDING
1. Flaps UP when taxiing.
2. Propeller HIGH PITCH.
3. Oil dilution as necessary.
4. Mixture IDLE CUT OFF.
5. SET brakes and LOCK controls.
6. All electrical switches OFF.

Revised 5-25-44
Supersedes Pilot's Check Lists of Previous Dates.

Pilot's Check List for virtually every World War Two USAAF and U.S. Navy Texan variant. (NAA)

BC-1s were among the first of the USAAC NA-16 derivatives to serve overseas with the Air Corps, and gear-up landings were not a Stateside novelty! Here, one of six BC-1s assigned to the Panama Canal Department (S/N 38-361) suffers the indignity of being trucked back to the Canal Zone from a Rio Hato landing on April 10, 1941. It was repaired and survived on into April 1944. (Jim Dias)

NORTH AMERICAN NA-16/AT-6/SNJ

BC-1s served throughout the United States during the war, this example (S/N 38-407 from the third batch of 92 aircraft) bears the unique Coffeyville, Kansas, twin stripes around the cowling, and displays the distinctive "chin" of the BC-1 in this 1942 view. (USAAF Coffeyville via David W. Ostrowski)

The CA-subvariants reflected a few slight local improvements. All the variants mounted two .303-caliber Mark V machine guns over the nose, a third gun (a Mark I) in the rear cockpit and a capacity of up to 1,000 pounds of bombs (1,500 pounds in the Wirraway III) on wing racks. Only practice bombs could be carried under the center section. The Wirraway was classified as a General Purpose aircraft, which covered a world of uses, including light/dive bombing, Army cooperation and coastal patrol, as well as advanced training. It was the first NA-16 derivative to see combat action, when aircraft of No. 12 Squadron at Darwin fielded their first examples in September (the British Commonwealth was at war with Germany and Italy long before the United States was pulled into the war), and the RAAF No. 21 (GP) Squadron flew that aircraft type on the Malayan Peninsula, seeing action against the Japanese there in December 1941.

NA-34

NAA Designation:	NA-16-4P
NAA Charge Number:	NA-34
Mfg. S/N:	34-389 to 34-418
User Regn. or S/N:	Argentine Army E.a.302 to E.a.331

Although NAA had been able to luxuriate in the substantial USAAC, U.S. Navy and foreign license production that arrived with some regularity through early 1937, no significant export production had been achieved at the home factory. This all changed when NAA received an order for at least 30 NA-16-4Ps. The order was Number AE-39 and was dated March 19, 1937.

These NA-16-4Ps were similar in many respects to the BT-9 series, but they had the standard armament of two over-the-nose, synchronized .30-caliber weapons and a flexible gun of the same caliber, and additional radio provision. The Argentine Army aircraft were fitted with the 420HP Wright R-975-E3 Whirlwind. The NA-16-4Ps were initially intended to serve as advanced trainers, but a number of them were later assigned to an Observation Group of the Argentine Army Aviation Command.

At least 15 of these sturdy aircraft remained in service with the Argentine Air Force until as late as January 1955. As noted earlier, the well-traveled demonstrator NA-18 was sold to Argentina at about the same time (the contract was actually dated April 5, 1937), but this aircraft had a Pratt & Whitney engine at the time of sale and was to serve as the pattern aircraft for a license-built variant. This did not happen, though.

BC-1s with warpaint are rare. Here S/N 38/359/"105," formerly of the 30th Fighter Squadron, Sixth Air Force, graces the ramp at Albrook Field, Canal Zone, in January 1945. It wasn't surveyed until June 1945, and it had been in Panama since 1938. (Col. Ole Griffith)

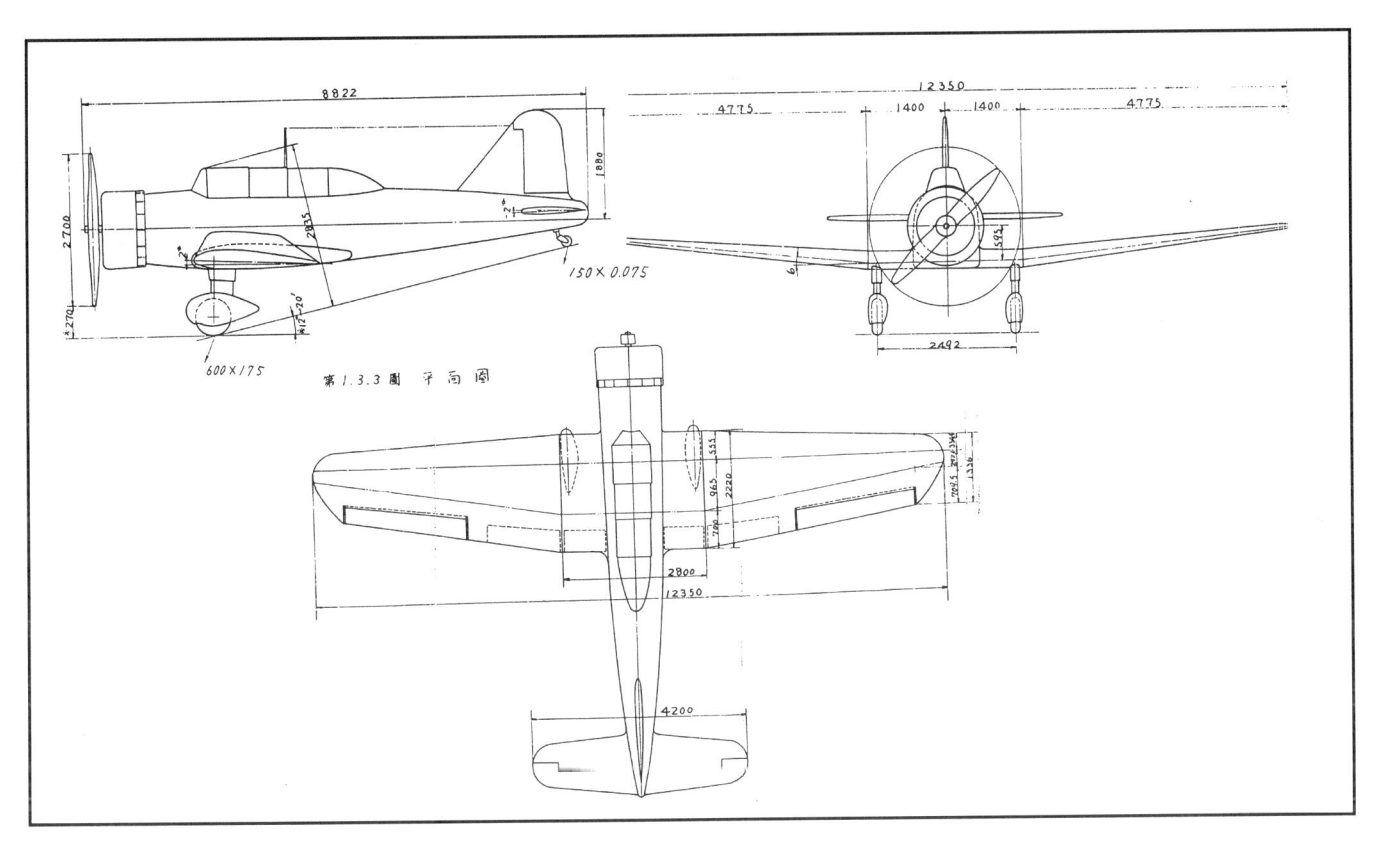

This three-view drawing of the Japanese Kyushu K10W1, alleged to be a "license-built NA-16-4R/NA-37," differs markedly from previously published line-drawings of the type. If anything, it bears a closer resemblance to the Vultee Model 54/BT-13 series. (Captured German/Japanese Technical Documents Microfilm, NASM)

NA-36 (BC-1)

NAA Designation:	(BC-1)
NAA Charge Number:	NA-36
Mfg. S/N:	36-420 to 36-504; 36-596 to 36-687
User Regn. or S/N:	AC37-416 to 37-456; 37-636 to 37-679 and AC38-356 to AC38-447

The NA-36 (BC-1) was the actual production version of the NA-26 cited earlier and heralded the first use of the new Air Corps type designation for a Basic Combat aircraft.

There has been some confusion over the manufacturer's serial numbers and Air Corps serial numbers assigned to these aircraft. The NAA *O Report*, often taken as gospel on the subject (as should be expected) reflects 85 BC-1s, Mfg. S/N 36-420 to 36-504, Air Corps serials 37-372 to 37-456, produced on Contract AC-9964 dated June 16, 1937. This contract was modified by Contract Change No. 2 to include an additional 92 identical aircraft, Mfg. S/N 36-596 to 36-687, Air Corps serials 38-356 to 38-447. The serials shown above, as derived directly from the Aircraft History Cards, are correct.

The sole NA-16-4R (NA-37), powered by a 450HP Pratt & Whitney R-985-9CG, was exported to Japan in September 1937, and it received the experimental Imperial Japanese Navy designation KXA1, Navy Experimental Type A Intermediate Trainer. (NAA 20.101/220 via Robert F. Dorr)

A front view of the Japanese NA-37 shows the three-bladed prop. It did not have armament provisions. (NAA 20.101/221 via Robert F. Dorr)

The first BC-1 was delivered to the Air Corps June 9, 1937, at a unit cost of $17,743.40, and was assigned to Wright Field. It was returned to North American on May 4, 1939, for unspecified reasons. It then returned to serve at Kelly Field, Texas, where it ended its days, but not before it was redesignated as a BC-1-I.

The BC-1 had several distinctive recognition features. Except for the first aircraft, which was delivered with a round-bottom rudder, like the NA-26 prototype for the series, the remainder had the larger, square-bottom rudder, which was similar to that used on the BT-9 and NJ-1. Additionally, and more significantly, the BC-1 had a large D/F loop on the underside of its forward fuselage. It was the first NA-16 family variant to define the basic shape of all that were to follow, and aside from the rudder, it is often identified by seasoned veterans as "an AT-6."

The BC-1 mounted a 500/550HP Pratt & Whitney R-1340-47 engine, which added yet another distinctive recognition feature to the type: the thin chin, running under the cowling from front to rear.

Oddly for a Basic Combat-type trainer, the BC-1 was not equipped to mount armament. When S/N 37-416 was exhaustively tested at Wright Field in May 1938, evaluators noted several alarming tendencies: First, during spin tests, the report noted "the airplane will not recover of its own accord," and, "rudder forces necessary for recovery are excessively high." Officers also noted that "there is severe buffeting on take-off just after the wheels have left the ground." However, and most interestingly, the report also stated that the aircraft could definitely be used for "other than design purposes."

Seldom mentioned is the fact that not fewer than 30 of these aircraft were redesignated as BC-1-I instrument trainers in January 1940 (the designation suffix being presented exactly as shown). The aircraft involved were 37-416, 432, 433, 437, 438, 444, 446, 447, 449, 637 to 640, 642, 650, 657, 666; 38-366, 374, 381, 382, 387, 389, 390, 400, 403, 424, 440, 441 and 445.

NA-37

NAA Designation:	NA-16-4R
NAA Charge Number:	NA-37
Mfg. S/N:	37-539
User Regn. or S/N:	(KXA1)

On August 31, 1937, Mitsubishi Jukogyo K.K. of Japan contracted for a single NA-16-4R powered by a 450HP Pratt & Whitney R-985-9CG engine driving a three-bladed prop, as well as the manufacturing rights to the design.

The aircraft was apparently deliv-

Although virtually every source claims the two NA-16s exported to Japan, along with a license to build them, led to the Kyushu K10W1 (Allied Code Name Oak), an examination of this K10W1 picture, taken post-war at the Omura seaplane base in October 1945, suggests only a superficial resemblance. (U.S. Marine Corps/Smeltzer via Bob Mikesh)

ered to Japan on or about November 15, 1937, and it was almost immediately turned over to the Imperial Japanese Navy, which evaluated it exhaustively under the designation KXA1, Navy Experimental Type A Intermediate Trainer.

Limited production of a highly modified version was then undertaken by K.K. Watanabe Tekkosho under the designation K10W1. The modified design incorporated revised vertical tail surfaces, among other changes, and was powered by the Japanese Nakajima Kotobuki 2 Kai air-cooled radial of 600HP. An examination of the accompanying photo and drawings from an actual Japanese manual reveals that the aircraft produced as the K10W1 seems to have borne little more than a passing resemblance to the NA-16, and it varies considerably from three-view drawings that were previously published in a number of otherwise authoritative sources purporting to represent the type. The instrument panel, similarly, bears little resemblance to any NAA panel I have found.

In any event, after completing 26 aircraft between 1941 and 1942, Watanabe handed over all tooling and engineering materials for the aircraft to Nippon Hikoki K.K., which delivered an additional 150 aircraft to the IJN between February 1943 and March 1944. Known to the Allies under the Recognition Code Name Oak, the K10W1s ironically supplanted the earlier, indigenous K5Y1 as the standard intermediate trainer in the Japanese Navy pilot training program.

The Chinese Nationalist Air Force ordered 35 NA-16-4s (NA-41s), which were virtually identical to USAAC BT-9Cs, but with two cowl guns. They were delivered in a dark brown overall camouflage that was unique to Chinese aircraft of the period. (NAA 20.201/115 via David W. Ostrowski)

NA-38

NAA DESIGNATION:	NA-16-4M
NAA CHARGE NUMBER:	NA-38
MFG. S/N:	38-540
USER REGN. OR S/N:	RSwAF 609

The single NA-38 was listed by NAA as "…identical to the NA-31," and it is a perfect case of two aircraft with the same NAA designation being ordered at different times and receiving completely different Charge Numbers. This aircraft was shipped disassembled to Sweden to aid in their license manufacture of the type. The contract was dated September 28, 1937.

The NA-38 had an unusual career. This solitary aircraft was often reported to have "never been assembled," and used only as a patterns aircraft. However, it was assembled in 1938 and delivered to the RSwAF in the spring of 1939 as the fifth Swedish production aircraft, with RSwAF serial 676.

Besides the NA-20 mentioned earlier, which was delivered to Honduras in 1937, the Hondurans also acquired two new NA-16-2As (NA-42s) in March 1938. They were painted in a distinctive service scheme: a dark blue fuselage, dove gray cheatline etched with gold, and dove gray wings and horizontal tail surfaces. The Hondurans declined to have NAA paint their rather elaborate coat of arms on the fuselage disc space provided, electing to render it themselves following delivery. (NAA 20.201/87 via Fred Freeman)

NORTH AMERICAN
NA-16/AT-6/SNJ

Incredibly, both the Honduran NA-20 and one of the NA-42s survived until as late as 1996. Here, marked in error as FAH 20, one of the two NA-42s, was completely refurbished (except for the discarded undercarriage pants) for the 50th anniversary of the FAH in 1979. The T-6D prop spinner is also an add-on nonstandard feature, and the radio mast aft of the canopy was added after delivery. (Dan Hagedorn)

The original order for Swedish-built Sk 14s (NA-16-4Ms) was for 35 aircraft. The original NA-38 was originally assigned to the F5 Wing (the RSwAF Flying School) and coded 5+115, but it later became 20+4, with the F20 Wing (the RSwAF Cadet School). It received a major inspection in August 1948, but it was destroyed at the RSwAF central shops in a fire on January 26, 1949, after a much more eventful life than has usually been ascribed to it.

NA-41

NAA Designation: NA-16-4
NAA Charge Number: NA-41
Mfg. S/N: NA-4141-697 to 41-731
User Regn. or S/N: Unknown

Described as "essentially the same as the USAAC BT-9C," the 35 NA-41s built for the Chinese Nationalist (Kuomintang) Government were covered by a contract dated February 23, 1938, and constituted NAA's second major export contract for the series. This order was attributed to the successful, earlier sales tour and demonstration of the Wright-powered NA-20. Apparently considered for a secondary tactical role, the aircraft had twin, synchronized .30-caliber machine guns over its nose and the standard, rear flexible gun of the same caliber. The NA-41s were shipped with an overall dark brown finish. Very little is known of their subsequent use in China.

NA-42

NAA Designation: NA-16-2A
NAA Charge Number: NA-42
Mfg. S/N: 42-691 and 42-692
User Regn. or S/N: Honduran Air Force s/n 21, 22

NAA described these two aircraft as "the same as the NA-20 but with armament," which is a rather odd statement, since the NA-20 that reached Honduras was every inch armament capable. The contract for the NA-42s were dated December 9, 1937, and the two aircraft were flight-delivered to Honduras on Export License No.4636, arriving March 4, 1938. These were the first aircraft manufactured and marketed by NAA that were actually described as "two-place fighters."

Both aircraft survived, alongside the NA-20, as late as June 30, 1957.

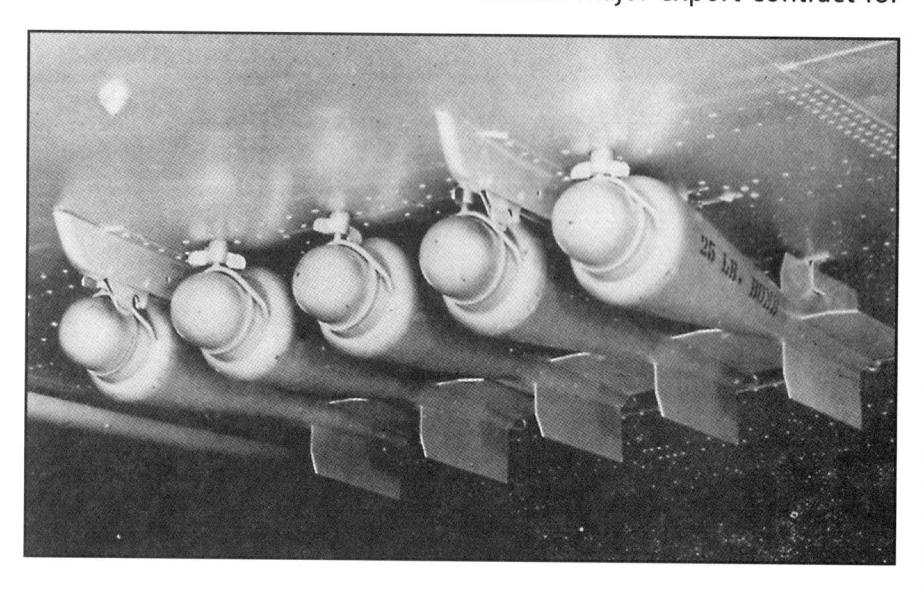

Starting in September 1938, NAA commenced a media blitz to market their new NA-44 'fighter,' multi-purpose aircraft. A truly robust variant, it mounted as many as four forward-firing guns, a flexible gun and various combinations of bombs. It featured a three-bladed prop and a 750HP Wright R-1820-F52 Cyclone engine. Here is an illustration of the installation of up to five 25-pound bombs under each wing. (NAA)

One, marked erroneously as S/N 20, was beautifully restored for the 50th anniversary of the Honduran Air Force in 1979. It remains on display in Honduras at the FAH officers club at Tegucigalpa's principle airfield. Both aircraft mounted the same 520HP Wasp that was found on the earlier NA-20.

NA-43

NAA Designation:	NA-16-1G
NAA Charge Number:	NA-43
Mfg. S/N:	—
User Regn. or S/N:	—

The Brazilian Army Air Force had reached an advanced stage of negotiations to purchase a series of NA-43s, which were similar to the BT-9C. They had actually reached the point at which a contract, dated December 9, 1937, was initiated, but the deal fell through when factions within the Brazilian Army ruled instead in favor of an order for 30 Stearman A76C3 and B76C3 multi-purpose biplane aircraft. The NA-43s would have been the Brazilian Army's first monoplane combat aircraft of modern vintage.

NA-44

NAA Designation:	NA-44
NAA Charge Number:	NA-44
Mfg. S/N:	44-747
User Regn. or S/N:	NX-18981, RCAF 3344

Perhaps the second most significant aircraft in the NA-16/Texan family tree after the ubiquitous NA-26, the sole NA-44 featured a semi-monocoque aluminum structure aft of the cockpit, unlike all the previous aircraft, which had been fabric-covered in that area. It also saw the first use of the smooth vertical fin and a 750HP Wright SG-1820-F52 Cyclone engine, the most potent powerplant to-date.

For its rather protracted demonstration tour, after it was registered in the Experimental series as NX-18981 and painted silver overall, the aircraft received a basic U.S. Army Air Corps blue fuselage and yellow wings (much like the NA-26).

Billed as a "light attack bomber dive bomber," the NA-44 was one of the fastest of the NA-16 developments, claiming a top speed of 250MPH. An expensively produced sales brochure, widely distributed to potential customers, advised that, besides the flexible rear gun, "four forward-firing guns could be fitted"—two synchronized and firing over the nose, and one in each wing—all of .30-caliber. Bomb racks on the outer wing panels could include up to four 100-pounders, 10 24-pounders or combinations.

This seminal aircraft was sold to the Royal Canadian Air Force (taken on

Demonstrated widely, the NA-44 was subsequently sold, along with the NA-26 to the Royal Canadian Air Force in August 1940, after bearing U.S. experimental license NX-18981 for some time. Allegedly called "Super Harvard" in RCAF service, it was unquestionably one of the fastest versions of the NA-16. (NAA 20.101/224 via David W. Ostrowski)

Contrary to many published reports, Venezuela acquired not one, but three NA-16-1GVs (NA-45s) in 1938. They were armament capable, and were finished in a forest green, except for the distinctive red, yellow and blue national insignia at four wing positions and the rudder. Instead of wing racks, they had four racks under the mid-fuselage section. (NAA 20.201/120 via Fred Freeman)

The Brazilian Navy acquired 12 NA-16-4 (NA-46) advanced trainers, final deliveries of six occurring in June 1940. Known locally as Perna Dura ("Stiff Legs"), they were colorfully marked, and all but two survived to pass to the Brazilian Air Force when the services were combined. The last one was stricken in 1958. (Sergio Luis dos Santos)

charge on August 6, 1940), painted in the then-current RCAF yellow trainer scheme and serialed RCAF 3344. It did not receive the Harvard type name, but according to one source, was sometimes referred to as the Super Harvard because of its large engine. It was assigned to the 2nd SFTS in 1940 and survived the war, and was finally struck off charge on February 20, 1947.

NA-45

NAA Designation:	NA-16-1GV
NAA Charge Number:	NA-45
Mfg. S/N:	45-693 to 45-695
User Regn. or S/N:	Venezuelan Air Force No.1 to 3

It is probable that these three aircraft (and the next 12 aircraft, the 12 NA-16-4s for the Brazilian Navy) were in actuality the first 15 aircraft of the canceled Brazilian Army NA-43 contract, which NAA had, perhaps over-confidently, already laid down.

The December 14, 1937, contract for these three aircraft described them as "basic combat general purpose planes," and they were the first essentially BC-1 style aircraft to be exported. They carried the standard array of two .30-caliber guns over the nose and a flexible rear gun, but had four A-3 bombs racks under the center section, rather than on the outer wing panels as on the NA-44. The NA-45s were the first Venezuelan service aircraft to feature retractable landing gear, and the aircraft proved to be something of a handful for the Venezuelan pilots.

One of the aircraft was written-off on June 9, 1938, crashing six miles from Maracay, its home base, and killing both occupants. One of these aircraft remained in service as late as June 1954, when U.S. intelligence reports described it rather cautiously as "a single AT-6A?"

NA-46

NAA Designation:	NA-16-4
NAA Charge Number:	NA-46
Mfg. S/N:	46-972 to 46-977; 46-1991 to 46-1996
User Regn. or S/N:	Brazilian Navy D1Na 192 to D1Na 203

It is not generally recognized that, prior to World War Two, Brazil had a well-developed Naval Aviation Corps, which in many respects, was better equipped and better trained than its Army counterparts of the time.

On December 2, 1938, the Brazilian Navy contracted for 12 NA-46 "BT-9C types" (which were so similar that they incorporated the fixed wingtip slots of the BT-9C), described as "advanced trainers."

A truly historic aircraft, this is the first NA-16-1E (NA-49), N7000, better known as the Harvard Mark I. Delivered to the RAF in December 1938, it did not enjoy a long service life. It was lost in a crash at Eyke, Suffolk, February 16, 1939. Here it is seen mounting a .303-caliber gun in the starboard wing. It was trainer yellow, except for the national insignia. (via David W. Ostrowski)

They were armament-capable, however, with the standard three-gun mix and bomb racks under the center section, exactly like the Venezuelan NA-45s. They also mounted a rather small D/F loop antennae under the forward fuselage.

In Brazilian Navy service, the aircraft was designated as D1Na and was given a "permanent" three-digit number, e.g., 192 to 203 (similar to a U.S. Navy Bureau of Aeronautics Number, which stayed with the aircraft). They also carried "unit" codes, such as 1-V-1. The aircraft were affectionately known in Brazilian service as Perna Duras ("Stiff Legs"). They served mainly with the 1a. Esquadrilha de Adestramento Militar at the Galeao Naval Air Base from October 1939, are were joined by the second batch of aircraft in April 1940.

All 12 of the aircraft survived in Navy service until the Naval Air Corps was integrated into the newly created *Forca Aerea Brasileira* in 1941. In 1945, the FAB began to use a designation system based on the USAAF system, and, ironically, the NA-46s received the designation BT-9 with FAB serials 1037 to 1047 (one aircraft had been lost in the interim). When the last NA-46 was finally struck off charge on March 7, 1958, it was certainly the last of its type in the world.

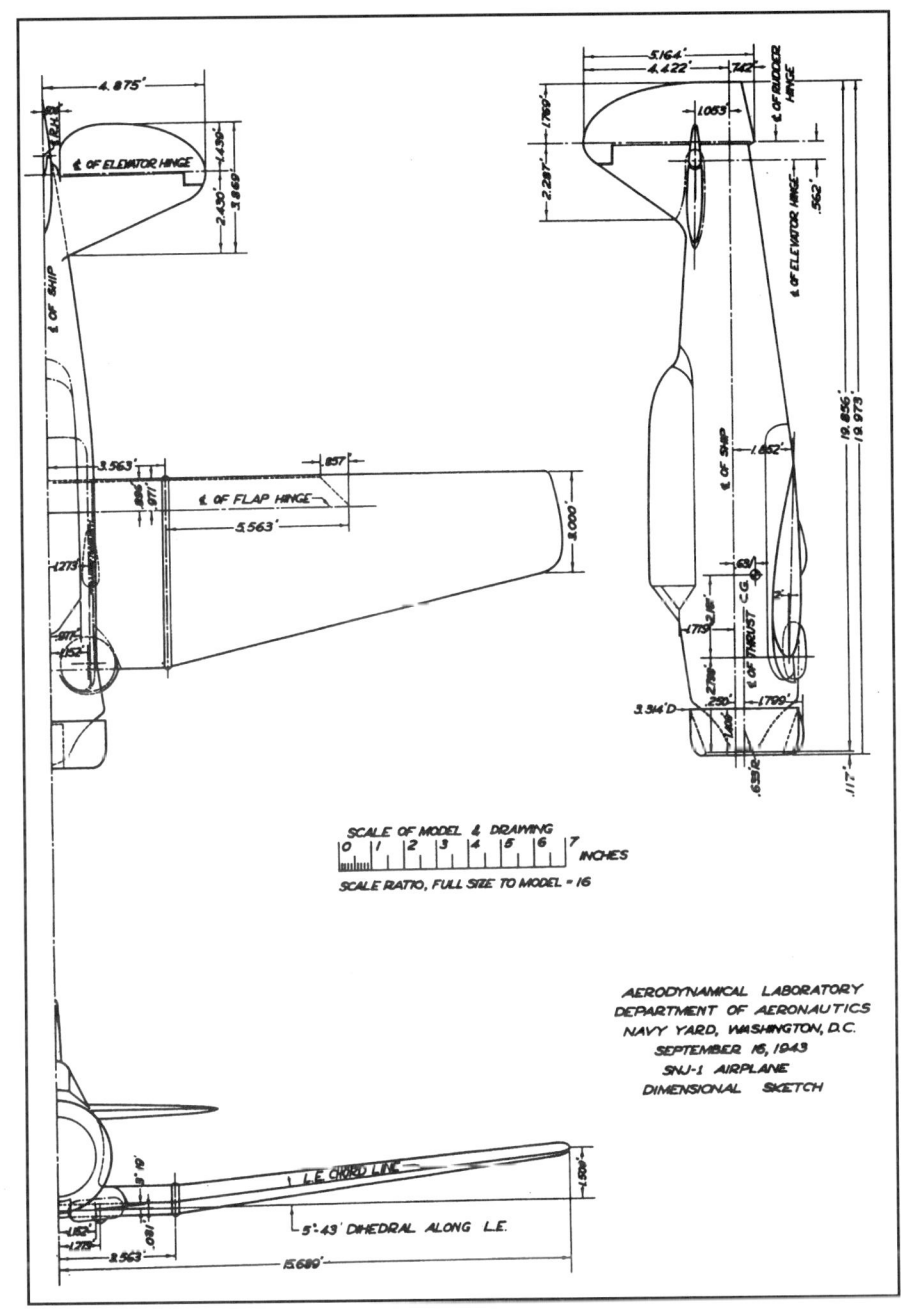

A September 1943 dimensional drawing of an SNJ-1 shows details of the dimensions, chord line and general planform. (USN)

NA-47

NAA Designation:	NA-16-4RW
NAA Charge Number:	NA-47
Mfg. S/N:	47-696
User Regn. or S/N:	Unknown

The second NA-16 design to be exported to Japan, the single NA-47 was otherwise identical to the earlier NA-37, but it had a smaller, Wright engine. It was ordered December 16, 1937, and was accepted by the Japanese (via Mitsubishi, disassembled) February 15, 1938, on contract MA-8070. One source states that the aircraft was shipped in parts as a pilot model for the license production of the K10W1.

NA-48

NAA Designation:	NA-16-3C
NAA Charge Number:	NA-48
Mfg. S/N:	48-732 to 48-746
User Regn. or S/N:	Unknown

The Chinese Nationalist Government ordered a second batch of NA-16s almost concurrent with the NA-41s noted earlier, with the NAA

Since the beginning of export marketing in 1935-36, North American had offered a "single-seat fighter" variant to prospective buyers. The first customer to actually take up this development, however, was the Peruvian Air Corps, which ordered seven NA-50s. These were delivered in 1939, and saw action during the 1941 war with Ecuador. So far as is known, these were the very first NA-16 developments to fire guns in anger. (NAA 20.201/192 and H.G. Martin via David W. Ostrowski)

Charge Number registered February 23, 1938. These 15 aircraft, however, were more akin to the Venezuelan NA-45s, as they featured four bomb racks under the center section and were in the NA-16-3 series (i.e., "two-place bombers") rather than the NA-16-4 ("advanced trainer") type of the earlier order. The first of these was accepted by Chinese representatives May 15, 1938, and the last in June 1938. Like the NA-41s, they were shipped to China sans markings, apparently painted the same shade of dark brown overall. Virtually nothing is known of their use in China.

NA-49 (HARVARD Mark I)

NAA DESIGNATION: NA-16-1E
NAA CHARGE NUMBER: NA-49
MFG. S/N: 49-748 to 49-947; 49-1053 to 49-1252
USER REGN. OR S/N: RAF N7000 to N7199; P5783 to P5982

Much has been written about the incredible pre-war buildup of the British Commonwealth forces. At home, the RAF concentrated primarily on producing combat aircraft, but it found in the North American NA-16 series a trainer that would gain immortality as the Harvard.

An initial order for 200 NA-49s, dated February 7, 1938, was quickly followed by another for 200 more. However, the first aircraft, N7000, did not arrive at the Aircraft and Armament Experimental Establishment (A&AEE) at Martlesham Heath, England, until December 1938. Once there, it was almost immediately subjected to a series of test flights to determine its flying characteristics and to enable publication of British "Pilots' Notes."

The second aircraft, N7001, joined the trials in January 1939, but the following month the Harvard Mark I's "tendency to spin" claimed N7000 as the first Harvard RAF victim when the aircraft crashed at Eyke, near Woodbridge in Suffolk, killing both occupants.

By then, however, Harvards were arriving on English shores in numbers and were issued to the Central Flying School and other Flying Training Schools with 12 FTSs at Grantham becoming the first. In September 1939, besides the FTSs, fighter operational training units also began receiving Harvards.

It is not generally known that some numbers of Harvard Mark I's were also dispatched, new, directly to Southern Rhodesia for use in the Empire Air Training Scheme (EATS), commencing as early as March

Although only three BC-2s (NA-54s) were acquired by the USAAC, they led most interesting lives. Here S/N 38-450 sits on the ramp at Albrook Field, Canal Zone, in 1945, following a long stint with the U.S. Military Mission to Chile, where its performance with a 600HP R-1340-45 engine had impressed the Chileans sufficiently to order 12 similar NA-74s. (Col. Ole Griffith)

The undercarriage layout of the BC-1A, which remained essentially unchanged throughout the AT-6, AT-6A, AT-6B and SNJ-3 series to come. (USAAF T.O. 01-60FC-2)

1940. Most of the last part of the second batch (P5916 to P5982) were shipped there directly from the United States, never seeing British skies, although some may have been transhipped via English ports as deck cargo. Mark Is remained in service in Southern Rhodesia until November 1945 and at least two examples that found their way to RAF units in the Mid-East were not stricken off charge until January 1947.

Some home-based RAF training units retained Mark Is as late as March 1946 and one Mark I, N7020, never left the United States, being retained for use by the British Purchasing Commission. Unlike other subsequent Harvards, none of these aircraft were sold overseas post-war or preserved, except three found in South Africa.

No finer testimonial to the overall value of the early Harvard can be found than that penned by none other than Sir Arthur Harris, GCB, OBE, AFC, in his book *Bomber Offensive* (New York, MacMillan, 1947). He wrote, "I was sent on a mission to America to buy aeroplanes. I took a technician and a test pilot with me... and Mr. Jimmy Weir came with us as an industrial expert to judge whether the factories to which we might propose to give our orders actually had the right equipment to enable them to carry them out. The result of this visit was the purchase of the first batches of Hudsons and Harvards. The Hudsons beyond doubt pulled us out of the soup when we used them for anti-submarine patrols in the first years of the war, and the Harvards broke the back of our problem in finding training aircraft."

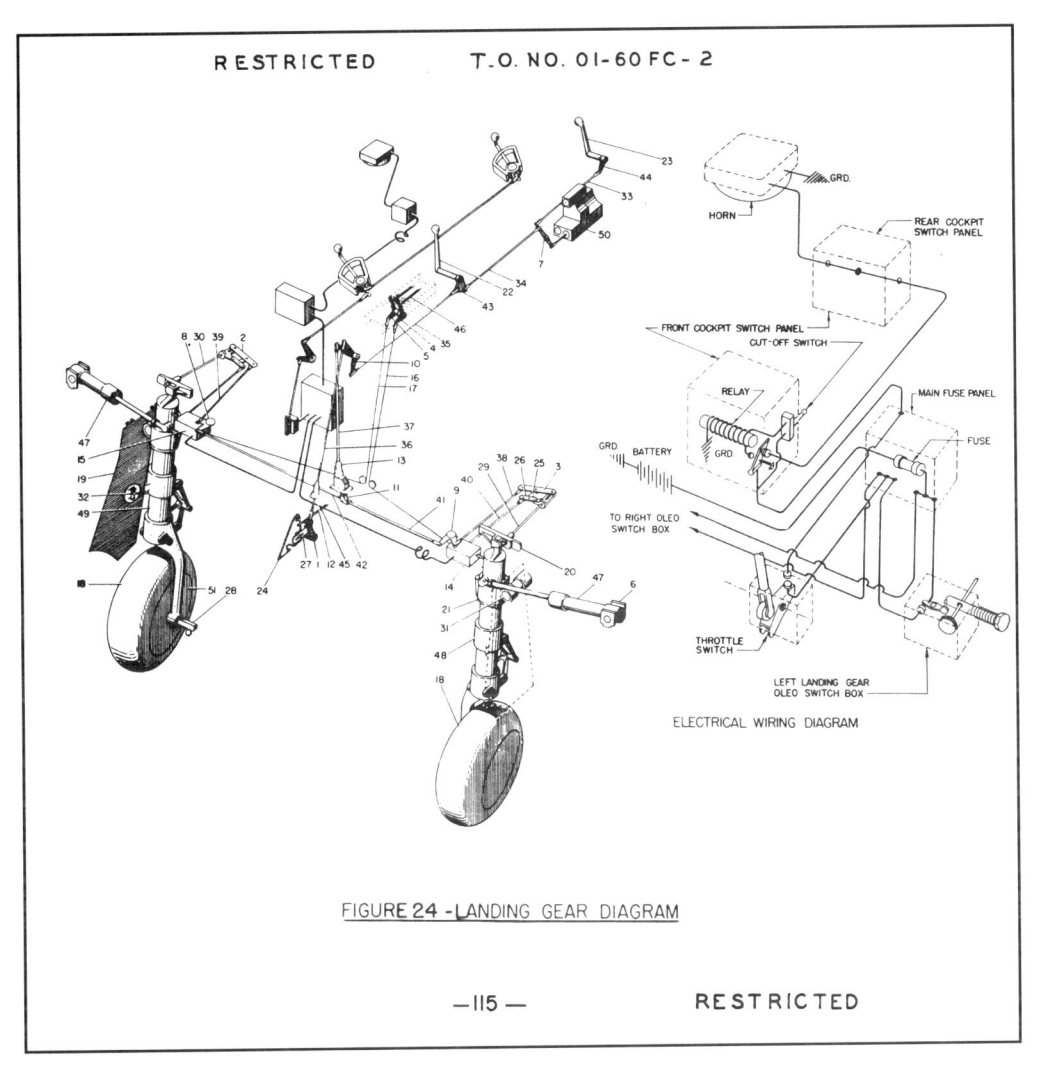

The Harvard Mark I used the 600HP Pratt & Whitney R-1340-S3H1 Wasp. The entire series of 400 aircraft were initially painted with the upper half of each fuselage standard RAF green-and-brown camouflage and the undersurfaces yellow.

NA-50

NAA Designation: NA-50
NAA Charge Number: NA-50
Mfg. S/N: 50-948 to 50-954
User Regn. or S/N: Peruvian Air Force XXI-41-1 to XXI-41-7 initially

Often described in error as NA-50As, the seven single-seat fighters built for the Peruvian Air Corps on Contract FO53169, dated August 1, 1938, were for all intents and purposes a development of the NA-16-5 concept as laid down originally in the NA-16 series. The seven aircraft completed flight testing at Inglewood in February 1939, and the first deliveries to Peru commenced in March.

NORTH AMERICAN NA-16/AT-6/SNJ

In these details of the cowling and prop of an Air Corps Reserve BC-1A, note that in the data block on the upper fuselage the serial number is preceded by the acronym A.C.R., a little known usage. (NAA 20.2130/218)

NA-50s saw action during the war with Ecuador in July 1941, and one was lost to ground fire. Four remained in service as late as June 1950, and incredibly, one still exists on a pylon at the main Peruvian Air Force base near Lima—a truly exotic survivor.

NA-52 (SNJ-1)

NAA Designation:	(SNJ-1)
NAA Charge Number:	NA-52
Mfg. S/N:	52-956 to 52-971
User Regn. or S/N:	Bu. No. 1552 to 1567

Similar in many respects to the Army Air Corps BC-1 (NA-36), but incorporating many of the improvements of the NA-44, the U.S. Navy acquired only 16 SNJ-1s on Contract No. 62916 dated September 23, 1938. The first one, Bu. No.1552, was accepted August 22, 1939, and assigned to NAS Anacostia.

The significance of the NA-50 is that NAA incorporated as many of the lessons learned in producing some 1,000 aircraft in the NA-16 series as possible into its design. It was promoted as "easy to maintain in the field," and had a comfortable and roomy cockpit for a single-seat fighter, with excellent visibility. The two internal fuel tanks incorporated Neobest and Neoseal protection against leakage and the 840HP Wright R-1820-G3 Cyclone gave the Peruvian NA-50s a top speed of 295HPH at 9,500 feet—very respectable for a Latin American fighter. Oddly, the aircraft mounted only two .30-caliber guns firing through the prop, but wing racks for up to 100 pound bombs were also fitted as standard.

Designated by the Navy as part of the new Scout Trainer category, for all intents and purposes, the SNJ-1 was basically an unarmed BC-1 with the NA-44's rear fuselage, a new wing, and the NA-50's square wingtip shape. They were natural metal except for the upper sides and around the leading edges of the wings, which were painted orange/yellow. Initially, the SNJ-1 grossed out at 4,807 pounds, compared to the 5,200 pounds of the SNJ-3/4, and it used the 500HP R-1340-6 engine. It is not generally recorded that, effective in April

As war once again loomed on the horizon, France ordered 230 NA-57s on February 21, 1939. These were similar to the much earlier NA-23 (BT-9B), but they incorporated improvements learned by NAA in the interim, as well as special equipment selected by the French. This was the second NA-57, which received the Armee de l'Air designation NAA 57-Et2. (NAA via David W. Ostrowski)

1940, most surviving SNJ-1s were re-engined with R-1340-18s.

NA-53

NAA Designation:	(NA-16-5)
NAA Charge Number:	NA-53
Mfg. S/N:	—
User Regn. or S/N:	—

Little is known about the canceled NA-53 single-seat fighter project, aside from the unsubstantiated report that it was intended as an inexpensive, single-seat fighter for an unspecified foreign government, possibly Nationalist China.

NA-54 (BC-2)

NAA Designation:	(BC-2)
NAA Charge Number:	NA-54
Mfg. S/N:	54-688 to 54-690
User Regn. or S/N:	USAAC 38-448 to 38-450

Only three BC-2s were ordered by the Army Air Corps, and oddly, were assigned a Charge Number of NA-54, ahead of that for the BC-1As (NA-55), on a different contract, AC9964, dated October 3, 1939.

In truth, these three aircraft were the final three NA-36s (BC-1s) that were modified to incorporate the advances of the pivotal NA-44. These included a 600HP R-1340-45 engine, three-bladed props, a metal-covered rear fuselage, rudder and wing tip shape changes and a geared engine. The BC-2s were the first USAAC aircraft in the series to look like the remainder of the AT-6 series to the casual observer.

These three aircraft led interesting careers, as related in my book *Alae Supra Canalem (Wings Over the Canal): The Sixth Air Force and Antilles Air Command* (Turner, Paducah, 1995, ISBN 1-56311-153-5). By early 1940, all three had been assigned to U.S. Air Mission use in Latin America, where they impressed our neighbors to the south with the qualities of the AT-6 series aircraft to follow. All three ended their days in the Sixth Air Force, and only one of them was ever assigned to the United States, albeit briefly, prior to the war.

NA-55-1 (BC-1A)

NAA Designation:	(BC-1A)
NAA Charge Number:	NA-55-1
Mfg. S/N:	55-1548 to 55-1630
User Regn. or S/N:	USAAC NG39-798 to 39-856; ACR40-707 to 40-716; NG40-717 to 40-725; ACR 40-726 to 40-739

Although designated as part of the Basic Combat series, and virtually identical to the BC-2 (NA-54), aside from the lack of a geared engine,

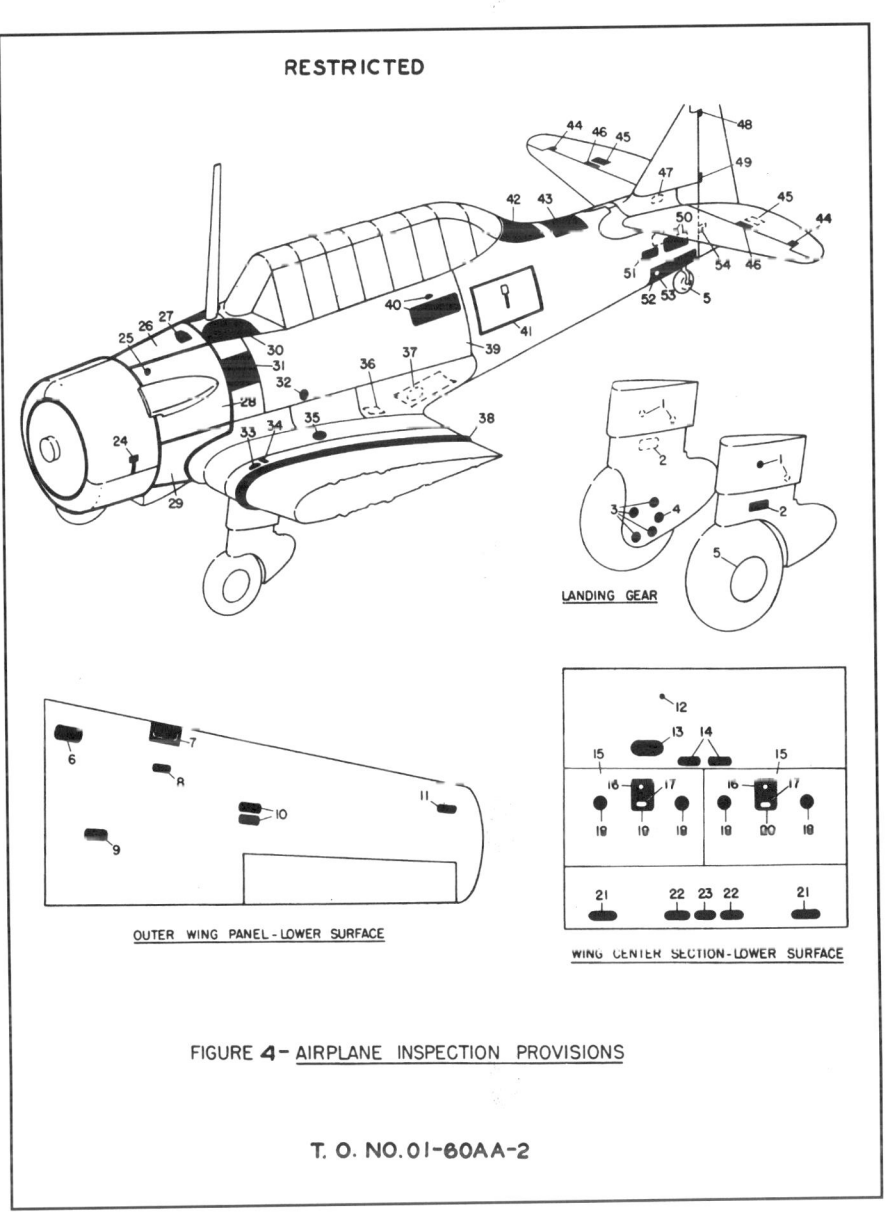

FIGURE 4 – AIRPLANE INSPECTION PROVISIONS

T. O. NO. 01-60AA-2

Details of the BT-14 aircraft inspection provisions, many of which were similar to other NA-16/BC/AT-6 variants. (USAAF T.O. 01-60AA-2)

the 83 BC-1As that were acquired in four distinct batches under Contract AC-12969 were intended for the Air Corps Reserve (ACR) and National Guard units, as reflected by the prefixes to their USAAC serial numbers.

The BC-1As were procured as a result of Circular Proposal C.P. 39-100 dated October 21, 1938, to which bids were submitted not only by NAA but also by the Aviation Manufacturing Corporation (Vultee Division) and Curtiss-Wright. It has not been hitherto reported that the actual NAA Charge Number for the BC-1A was not NA-55, but, rather NA-55-1, one of the few known uses of a suffix to an NAA Charge Number.

The first five aircraft were equipped with the R-1340-47 engine, which had the same power rating as the remaining examples that mounted the R-1340-49, but in spite of the Basic Combat designation, these aircraft were intended, in the words of the actual NAA "Detail Model Specification," "to be used for a tactical mission; to provide a means for command liaison and reconnaissance for Corps and Divisions, and to provide for the maintenance of the combat flying proficiency of pilots and observers."

The BC-1A could mount two .30-caliber guns: one M-2 over the nose, synchronized, and the flexible gun (also an M-2) in the rear. It had no bomb-carrying capability whatsoever. A Type N-2A optical gun sight was provided for the pilot.

To the casual observer, the BC-1A appeared identical to the final form that nearly every subsequent U.S. Army Air Corps version of the AT-6 would take. A recognition feature, however, was the large D/F loop under the forward fuselage between the wheel wells.

One source alleges that the original serial number range for the BC-1As was to have gone through number 40-740, but this last aircraft was canceled in favor of the AT-6-NA designation. In fact, the last nine BC-1As in the National Guard block were apparently completed as AT-6s (S/N 40-717 to 40-725) in addition to the last aircraft noted (#40-740).

One source claims that a single BC-1A was fitted with an AT-6A center section and designated as the BC-1B, but I could locate no such designation in the Individual Aircraft History Cards.

Surprisingly, a few BC-1As survived to be surplused at the end of the war, and small numbers found their way into foreign air arms, with Peru and Sweden acquiring one each.

NA-56

NAA Designation:	NA-16-4
NAA Charge Number:	NA-56
Mfg. S/N:	56-1453 to 56-1502
User Regn. or S/N:	Chinese Air Force

The NA-56, like the other orders from China, poses some interesting historical contradictions. The NAA *O Report* states unequivocally that China ordered a total of 50 of these aircraft on a contract dated April 18, 1939, and that they were "basically the same as the NA-55 (i.e., USAAC BC-1A) but with fixed gear." While photos appear to bear this out, there also appear to be significant differences in the engine and cowling that have not been documented.

However, another NAA document states that only five NA-56 general purpose aircraft were acquired by China, with the order placed on April 15, 1940, and final acceptance was taken in August 1940. While it is possible that this may have been a follow-on order to the initial batch of 50, nothing further has surfaced on any of these aircraft.

A rare bird: Few BT-14s received warpaint, and the circumstances of this otherwise anonymous BT-14 acquiring same are unknown. (via David W. Ostrowski)

NA-57

NAA Designation: NA-57 (BT-9B)
NAA Charge Number: NA-57
Mfg. S/N: 57-1253 to 57-1452;
57-1518 to 57-1547
User Regn. or S/N: French Air Force NAA 57-Et2 1 to NAA 57-Et2 230

Often confused with the later NA-64 (230 of which were also ordered by the French) the NA-57s were essentially NA-23s with certain improvements specified by the French, including the reverse action of the throttle which the French preferred. These aircraft had 420HP Wright R-975-E3 engines.

Contrary to popular belief, all but 16 of the 230 NA-57s, contracted for on February 21, 1939, reached French territory (although about 40 of them were apparently stopped in transit at Casablanca where disembarkation and assembly provisions were inadequate). Those that reached France were assembled by SNCAO at Nantes. None of this variant were taken over by the British RAF as is so often suggested. Unfortunately for posterity, the opposition (the German Luftwaffe) did acquire a considerable number of NA-57s (the best estimate is 50 aircraft) that were seized when the Vichy French Air Force was demobilized November 27, 1942.

The NA-57 represented North Americans largest single contract as of that date, not counting the British Harvard Mark I order of two batches of 200 each. Not previously recorded is the fact that, although most of the NA-57s bore the French basic trainer designation of NAA 57 Et 2 on the rudder, a few also had the designation NAA 57 P 2. Some sources claim that this indicated a secondary photographic mission capability, like the later NA-64s. However, another source claims that the NAA 57 P 2s were intended for use as conversion trainers. At least one, and probably more, are known to have been camouflaged in a scheme similar to that seen on other French Air Force aircraft early in the war, suggesting something more than a trainer role.

It is seldom noted that the first 30 aircraft of this series actually served with the French Navy, receiving their serials U-416 to U-445. The final 16 aircraft, stranded in the United States as of the French surrender in June 1940, went to the RCAF as Yales Is.

NA-58 (BT-14 and BT-14A)

NAA Designation: (BT-14)
NAA Charge Number: NA-58
Mfg. S/N: 58-1655 to 58-1905
User Regn. or S/N: AC40-1110 to 40-1360

Of the entire NA-16 family, the BT-14 was probably the easiest variant to distinguish from others. The BT-14 is similar to the earlier NA 23, especially the one-off BT-9D, and incorporates wings and empennage that are similar to the BC-1A. The BT-14's fuselage was 14 inches longer than the BT-9, and the 251 BT-14s had a rather distinctive downward curve over the nose—its chief recognition feature.

The contract for the BT-14s wasn't signed until April 23, 1939, which was the same date as the contract for the first 94 genuine AT-6s. NAA assembly lines at Inglewood late in June 1940 (at which time the total order was 60 percent complete) were only then beginning to concentrate exclusively on these aircraft, along with export orders for variants of the NA-16 for the British Commonwealth, Brazil, Thailand and Venezuela. The BT-14 was the last of the fixed-gear NA-16 derivatives built for the Army Air Corps. The first one, S/N 40-1110 was delivered September 9, 1939, to Wright Field, and never left there, as it was wrecked near the field on September 7, 1942.

When 27 surviving aircraft were re-engined in 1941 with the 400HP R-985-11 engine, they were retroactively redesignated BT-14A-NAs.

By 1943, the colorful pre-war blue and yellow USAAC trainer colors were long-gone, but sometimes the clean up of these wasn't all it could have been. (Martin and Kelman via David W. Ostrowski)

NORTH AMERICAN NA-16/AT-6/SNJ

Design Maturity

THE AT-6 AND WORLD WAR TWO VARIANTS

The contract for the first aircraft to bear the designation AT-6 was dated April 28, 1939, a scant six months ahead of the German invasion of Poland on September 1, 1939, and the beginning of what was to become known as World War Two.

NA-59 (AT-6)

NAA DESIGNATION: (AT-6-NA)
NAA CHARGE NUMBER: NA-59
MFG. S/N: 59-1631 to 59-1639;
59-1906 to 59-1990
USER REGN. OR S/N: AC40-717 to
40-725; 40-2080 to 40-2164

The Air Corps had appreciated that the Basic Combat designation assigned to the NA-54s and NA-55s were something of a misnomer. Although given that they were intended initially for issuance primarily to Air Corps Reserve and National Guard units to maintain proficiency, rather than the organic Air Corps training establishment, the designation wasn't too far off the mark.

The next batch of virtually identical aircraft, however, were indeed intended for Active Duty training, and as a consequence, the Air Corps re-activated the old AT for "Advanced Training" designation series that had not been used since 1928, thus arriving at the AT-6 (no suffix).

Strictly speaking, these 94 aircraft were a continuation of the BC-1A contract (AC-12969), merely using a different designation; the aircraft were identical aside from very minor modifications. In fact, the first nine AT-6s (40-717 to 40-725) were actually NA-55s completed and designated as AT-6s. However, things are sometimes not as they appear. One of the chief recognition features of the BC-1A was the large D/F loop under its forward fuselage. The USAAF muddied the waters in late May 1943 when it authorized the Army Air Forces Instructor School (Instrument Pilot) at Bryan, Texas, to modify some 170 various AT-6 variants on the base by adding a rotatable loop on the aircraft. Aircraft recognition experts beware!

The first AT-6, S/N 40-717, was delivered June 24, 1939, and was assigned briefly to Bolling Field, DC. It then moved to the U.S. Military Mission at Ottawa, Canada, where it spent the rest of the war, not returning to the United States until April 8, 1944. Appropriately, the first AT-6 was also the first example of the breed to leave the continental United States.

The AT-6 was powered by the 600HP Wright R-1340-47 and could mount only two .30-caliber machine guns: one over the starboard nose (synchronized) and a flexible gun in the rear cockpit.

The USAAC commenced, through necessity, to add block numbering and manufacturer/location suffixes to their designation procedures as early as 1939. The AT-6s in some instances were recorded in documentation (and on the "data block"

The second aircraft in the second batch of AT-6s, 40-2081 displays the definitive lines of the series in this great in-air view. The ADF tear drop under the forward fuselage isn't obvious. The aircraft had been accepted by the USAAC March 31, 1940, and was initially assigned to Kelly Field, moving to Randolph in May 1941. It survived the war to be offered for surplus in October 1945. (via David W. Ostrowski)

under the cockpit on the left side) as AT-6-NA, indicating that they had been built by North American (Inglewood).

NA-61

NAA Designation: NA-16-1E
NAA Charge Number: NA-61
Mfg. S/N: 61-1503 to 61-1517; 61-1640 to 61-1654
User Regn. or S/N: RCAF 1321 to 1335; RCAF 1336 to 1350

On May 25, 1939, the Royal Canadian Air Force ordered 30 NA-16-1Es, which were virtually identical to the NA-49 Harvard Mark Is ordered in February 1938 for the British RAF.

These aircraft were not identified in NAA records as Harvard Mark Is and the aircraft had nothing to do with the British order for almost identical aircraft. It wasn't until some time later that these aircraft, for Commonwealth conformity, were also designated as Harvard Is within the RCAF. Due to its extremes of weather, the RCAF was the first service to test the NA-16 on skis. Although Noorduyn produced 34 sets to mount on this first RCAF order of NA-16s, only serial number 1321 was ever actually mounted with them. An experimental "heat muff" exhaust system was also tested successfully on one of these aircraft, these becoming a common feature on later RCAF aircraft and a prime recognition feature of Canadian NA-16s/Harvards.

The first NA-61 was delivered to the RCAF on July 20, 1939, and remarkably, was one of two from this first batch to survive the entire war. Both survivors were stricken on May 9, 1946.

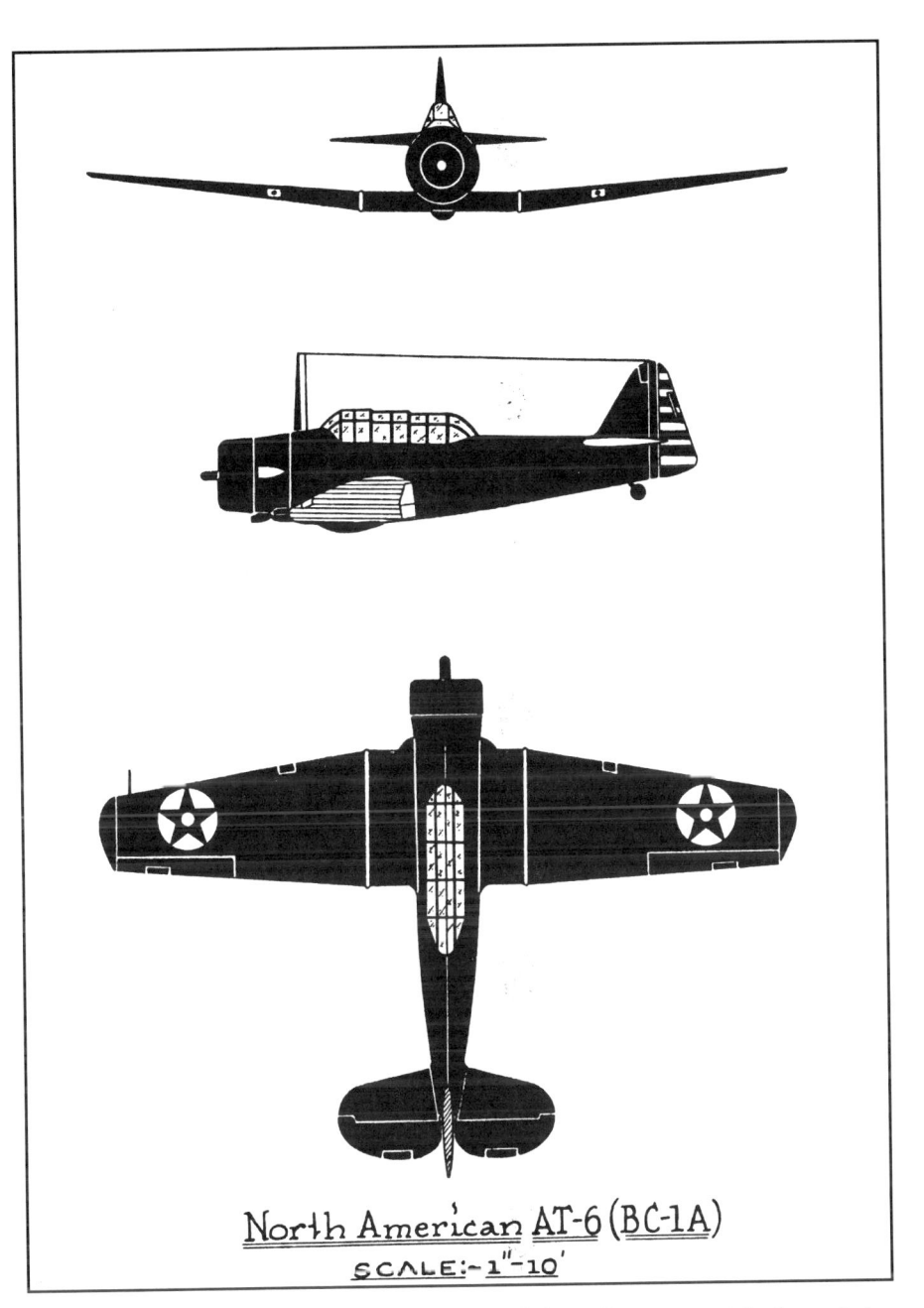

At last, the AT 6 (NA 59). A comparison of this silhouette with that of the earlier issue showing the BC-1A and AT-6 reveals that an air intake has been added on the port (left) side of the forward fuselage and that the RDF loop has been dropped from the lower fuselage. Also note the subtle changes in the canopy framing. (USAAC)

NA-64

NAA Designation: NA-64
NAA Charge Number: NA-64
Mfg. S/N: 64-2033 to 64-2232; 64-3018 to 64-3047
User Regn. or S/N: French Air Force NAA 64P-2 No.1 to 230

Still scurrying to rearm and re-equip her Air Force and Naval Air Arm, the French placed a follow-on order for an additional 230 aircraft that were very similar to the earlier NA-57s they had ordered, but they incorporated some of the improvements of the NA-58 (BT-14). Initially, the order had been 200, although

This early AT-6 was assigned to the 50th Pursuit Group out of Selfridge Field late in 1940. (Leo J. Kohn)

French sources quote the odd total of 199, but increased. Chief among these improvements was an all-metal fuselage, newly designed wings and empennage units, and Pratt & Whitney R-985-25 engines, unlike the previous Wright-powered NA-57s. The first NA-64 was test flown at Inglewood on February 12, 1940, and NAA was optimistically advising the press that "shipments are well in advance of contract requirements," little knowing that time was running out for the *Armee de l'Air*. Of the total ordered, only 111 were actually charged to the French.

The remaining 118 aircraft (often given as 119) are usually cited as having been "taken over by Britain," but they were delivered to the Royal Canadian Air Force as the North American Yale I, a fact seldom recognized in the origin of these aircraft. These Yale I aircraft received RCAF serials 3346 to 3463, and included a wide range of Mfg. S/Ns from the original French contract—from a low of 64-2118 to a high of 64-3047. They were taken up by the RCAF between August 23 and September 27, 1940, and the last examples were stricken October 1, 1946. Confusingly, it is almost certain that the last 16 NA-57s from the earlier contract were also taken up by the RCAF, and called Yale Is, but these have not been positively linked to any known RCAF serial numbers.

These French NA-64s, unlike most of the NA-57s, were originally intended for a secondary tactical photographic aircraft role, hence the "P-2" designation after the type presentation in French practice. Their primary function, however, remained as basic trainers. The first aircraft in this series carried U.S. experimental civil registration NX-13397.

Some of the NA-64s were destined for the Aeronaval, the French Naval Aviation organization, but it is not clear if any actually made it. Like the NA-57s, many of these aircraft were seized by the Luftwaffe when Vichy was overrun. According to French sources, a total of 341 NA-57s and NA-64s reached France, and a combined total of 49 survived to pass into the Vichy French Air Force. Of those which arrived in French territory, at least 100 served in French North Africa, and it may be assumed that some survived the Allied landings there.

While NAA was hustling trying to fill ever increasing U.S. military and export orders, the Canadians weighed in with an order of their own on May 25, 1939, for 30 NA-16-1Es (NA-61s). Initially, these were flown as they were completed to Canada. However, when the U.S. invoked the Neutrality Act, the finished aircraft were flown to the border at Coutts, Alberta (and other points), and literally pushed across! RCAF S/N 1321 (the serial under the leading edge of the wing is reversed) was the first NA-61, which the RCAF designated as Harvard I. It was delivered July 19, 1939, and survived the war. During its career, this aircraft was fitted with fixed struts and skis for winter operations. (NAA 20.201/224)

NA-65 (SNJ-2)

NAA Designation: (SNJ-2)
NAA Charge Number: NA-65
Mfg. S/N: 65-1997 to 65-2032
User Regn. or S/N: Bu. No. 2008 to 2043

The first of two distinctly different batches of aircraft to receive the designation SNJ-2 by the U.S. Navy, this first increment of 36 aircraft were similar to the earlier NA-52 (SNJ-1) but they incorporated many of the features of the NA-55-1 (BC-1A). Principal differences were a greater wing span (42'7", with a corresponding increase in wing area to 258.6 square feet) and a new gross weight of 4,954 pounds. They also adopted the R-1340-36 engine, and did not have any armament installation capability.

Some of the aircraft in this first batch of SNJ-2s were among the last USN aircraft to use the old vertical red, white and blue rudder stripes of the pre-war period. The SNJ-2 was also the fastest of the SNJ-1/2/3/4 series, with a maximum speed of 213 MPH at 6,000 feet. By July 1941, most of this initial series of SNJ-2s was assigned to Pensacola and Miami. A key recognition feature was the hump under the forward fuselage just aft of the wheel wells, which covered the fuel transfer gear.

Many SNJ-2s survived the war, and by 1947, some surplus examples in civil hands were being advertised for sale for as little as $1,875 with but 2,280 hours total time. Foreign military use of SNJ-2s was limited, although the Royal Swedish Air Force acquired at least two surplus in 1953.

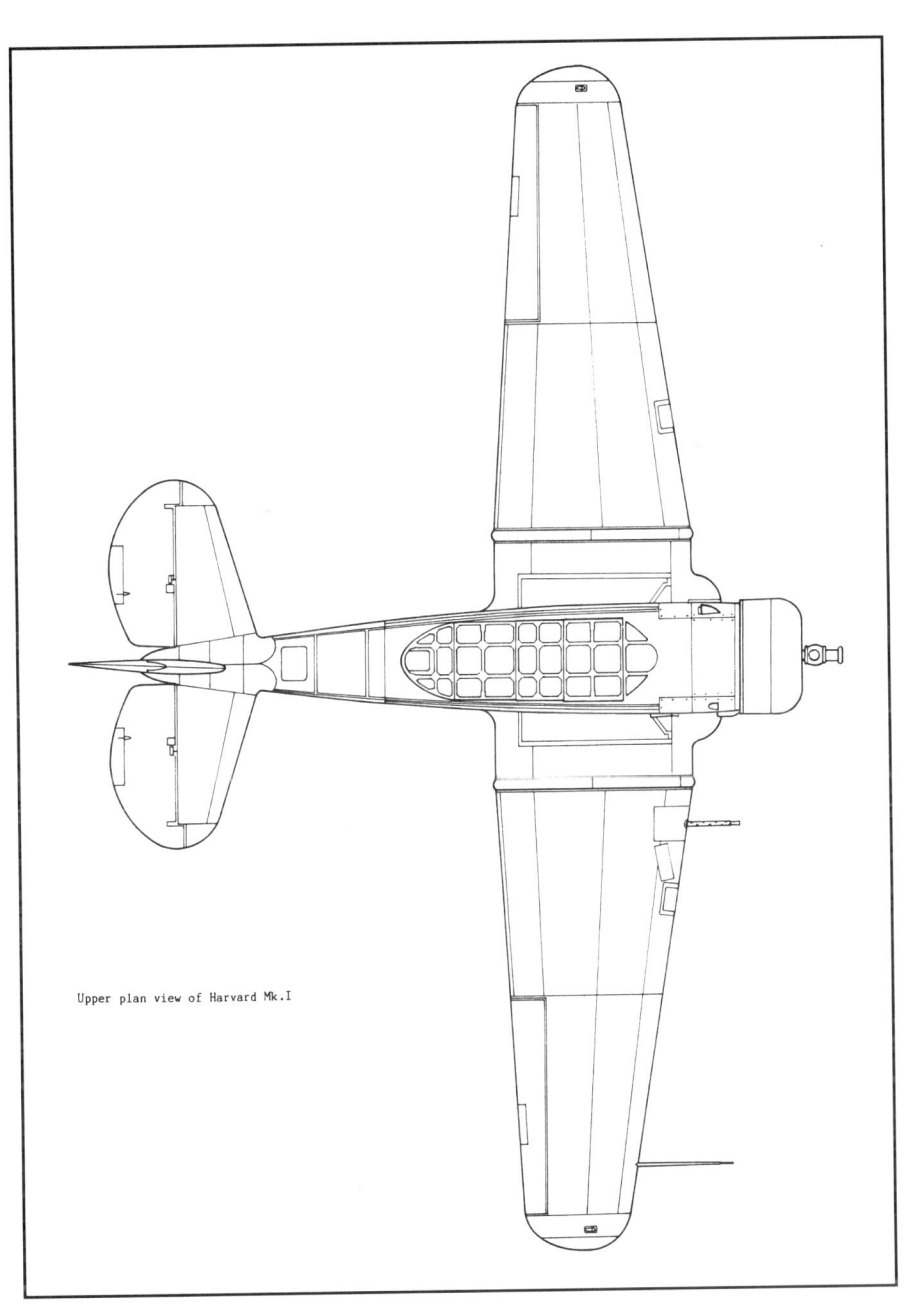

This overhead view of a British Harvard I, when compared with the similar overhead view of the Harvard II, IIa, IIb and III, illustrates the significant differences between the two major variants. (Courtesy of Air-Britain Historians, Ltd.)

NA-66 (HARVARD Mark II)

NAA Designation: (Harvard Mark II)
NAA Charge Number: NA-66
Mfg. S/N: 66-2234 to 66-2833
User Regn. or S/N: RCAF 2501 to 3013; RAF AH185 to AH205+; RNZAF NZ901 to NZ967

Often poorly understood, the 600 aircraft order for Harvard IIs (sometimes cited as "NA-66 Modified Harvards" or "NA-66 Harvard (Modified)" in NAA documents) was more complex, in terms of end-users, than has often been depicted. By October 1940, when withdrawal of the Harvard Mark Is from service in the United Kingdom was taking place, eight Mark II aircraft with

Besides the earlier NA-57s, the French also ordered 230 NA-64s, which were similar to the NA-57s but incorporated some BT-14 (NA-58) improvements including an all-metal fuselage. Of these, 119 never reached France. The first NA-64 carried U.S. experimental license NX 13397 during tests. (NAA 64-0-1 via David W. Ostrowski)

serials in the BD130 to BD137 (ex-RCAF serials 2521 to 2528) arrived to supplement them. At the same time, the first of 20 aircraft, carrying RAF AH serials, was received in Canada for use in the new Commonwealth Air Training Scheme.

The Mark IIs in the United Kingdom were used for only a short time, however, before five of them were shipped to Southern Rhodesia (along with the Mark Is). Two of the others were handed over at some point to the Eighth Air Force when it arrived in England. Six more Mark IIs, carrying BJ or BS serials, which arrived in the UK in November 1940, saw little or no service there and were sent on to Rhodesia (although six of this batch were lost at sea when the transport they were aboard was sunk).

Bulk deliveries of Mark IIs began to Canada in July 1941 following the first flight of the type at Inglewood in May 1940 and continued on into May 1942. Three hundred and five Mark IIs were received there by this time, bearing RAF serials in the AH, AJ, BW and RCAF ranges. They were allocated to the large number of Service Flying Training Schools (SFTSs) in Canada and operated right alongside the RCAF examples. By October 1944, the SFTSs administered by the RAF had all closed down, and the surviving RAF-serialed Harvard IIs were taken over by the RCAF, creating thereby many puzzles for aero historians in years to come!

A further 103 Mark IIs were shipped to Southern Rhodesia (via South Africa) from August 1941, and by the end of the war, not less than 40 of these had been written off in training accidents. Twelve survived to be sold to the new Southern Rhodesian Air Force in February 1949.

Forty-seven Mark IIs were shipped to the Middle East, where they enjoyed only a brief service life in sundry roles while four that went to India had all been lost to accidents by November 1943. Finally, 38 Mark IIs were shipped directly from NAA to the Royal New Zealand Air Force (at their own expense), as shown in the serials list.

The recognition differences between the Harvard Mark I and Mark II were almost entirely structural. The rounded wing tips of the Mark I were replaced by square-tips

The U.S. Navy bought 36 SNJ-2s (NA-65s) on a contract let in September 1939, just as things started coming apart in Europe. Here, Bu. No. 2016 is shown while assigned to the "Commander Aircraft Scouting Force," its first assignment. This ninth production example was stricken at Corpus Christi, Texas, on August 8, 1946. (via David W. Ostrowski)

A few SNJ-2s even received warpaint like this unidentified example that was photographed sometime after August 1943. (USAAC via David W. Ostrowski)

on the Mark II and the rounded trailing-edge of the rudder of the Mark I was dropped in favor of a straight inclined trailing-edge on the Mark II. The rear fuselage was also a semi-monocoque aluminum alloy section and had metal side-panels in the front fuselage section, similar to the BC-1A. The engine, in both cases, was the Pratt & Whitney R-1340-S3H1 Wasp. On the Mark II, the exhaust pipe extended back as far as the cockpit on the starboard side, just clearing the top surface of the wing.

For the record, 15 other Harvard Mark IIs originally built and allocated RCAF serial numbers later gained RAF serials, besides those noted earlier. These were:

BJ410 and BJ411 ex-RCAF 2529 and 2530

BJ412 to BJ415 ex-RCAF 2534 to 2537

BS808 ex-RCAF 2538

DG432 to DG439 ex-RCAF 2539 to 2546 (six of these eight aircraft were lost at sea in transit)

Post-war, a few ex-RCAF Harvard IIs found their way into service with the Royal Swedish Air Force via surplus channels.

NA-68 (P-64)

NAA Designation: NA-50A (P-64)
NAA Charge Number: NA-68
Mfg. S/N: 68-3058 to 68-3063
User Regn. or S/N: USAAC 41-19082 to 41-19087

These six aircraft, similar in many respects to the earlier NA-50s delivered to Peru, were ordered for the Royal Thai Air Force, and were in fact ready to be shipped—complete with RTAF camouflage—when they were acquired by the U.S. Government, along with the NA-69s that had also been ordered by Thailand.

More heavily armed than the Peruvian NA-50s, with a redesigned empennage and canopy structure, the NA-68s were incorporated into the USAAC and given the "pursuit" designation P-64. Designed to accommodate two .30-caliber guns over the nose, two more in the wings, and a 20mm cannon in each of two underwing pods, plus racks for a ventral 550-pound bomb or two 110 pounders under the wings, the USAAC ultimately deleted the armament and utilized the aircraft as hacks and fighter-trainers in a rather desultory manner.

The 36 Navy SNJ-2s were similar to the earlier SNJ-1s (NA-52) but benefitted from some of the improvements of the Army's BC-1A (NA-55). This is Bu. No. 2025 while assigned to Naval Reserve Air Base Oakland. It had been accepted June 5, 1940, and as of August 1941 was assigned to VT-3 (USS Saratoga). It later served with OTU VF-6, and was finally stricken on March 31, 1946. (Shertzer via Peter M. Bowers)

NORTH AMERICAN NA-16/AT-6/SNJ

51

Of the 600 Harvard IIs (NA-66s) initially ordered for use by RAF, Royal Canadian and Royal New Zealand Air Force training elements, two crashed before delivery. This RCAF example, S/N 2660 (C/N 66-2393) was delivered in November 1940 and served until it was wrecked in August 1955. The exhaust shroud was a key recognition feature, otherwise they were virtually identical to the USAAC AT-6 (NA-59). (RCAF via Robert F. Dorr)

NA-69 (A-27)

NAA Designation:	NA-44 (A-27)
NAA Charge Number:	NA-69
Mfg. S/N:	69-3064 to 69-3073
User Regn. or S/N:	USAAC 41-18890 to 41-18899

Together with the NA-68 single-seat fighters, which had also been ordered by Thailand (often quoted in error as Siam—the nation had used the name Thailand from 1939) on November 30, 1939, the 10 NA-44s were the first NA-16 derivatives actually described by NAA as "attack bombers." The NA-69s could mount four forward-firing 7.7mm-caliber weapons (two over the nose and one in each wing), plus the flexible rear gun and center-line bomb racks, plus attach points for other bombs under the outer wing panels (totaling up to 400 pounds).

The NA-69 was powered by the 745HP Wright R-1820-75 Cyclone engine and the first example was test flown in late June 1940. Like the NA-68s, though, these never reached Thailand. They had been shipped as far as Manila in the Philippines (the six NA-68s were still at the NAA plant) when a flurry of telegrams, the earliest dated January 14, 1941, advising of "preliminary negotiations leading to the *purchase* [emphasis authors] of the aircraft, plus spares for both types" started flying between Washington, NAA and the PI. The NA-68s had been procured for the RTAF by the agency of the Aerial Transport Co., but although actually in transit in the Philippines, the U.S. State Department had refused an export license. This had been precipitated by the appearance of the Japanese in Indo-China in 1940 and the Thai accommodation with them, which led to their repossession (by force) of the former Laotian provinces of Thailand that had been ceded to the French in 1893.

The NA-69s, however, were anything but "combat ready" aircraft. While they were fitted with two synchronized guns over the nose, through an "oversight" by the engine manufacturer, Wright, this gear had plunger housings with threads that would not permit the solenoid to seat properly, hence the guns could not be fired. Wright shipped the correct plungers to the RTAF via Pan Am air freight (certainly one of the first such instances of "rush" arms shipment), believing that the necessary corrections would be made in Thailand.

Bearing post-war RCAF markings, S/N 3062 had served since July 1941 but it was written off at Sea Island on March 14, 1953. In this view, it displays the radio mast and RDF bullet installation unique to RCAF post-war Harvards. (via David W. Ostrowski)

52

WARBIRDTECH
SERIES

Both the NA-68s and NA-69s, in the final analysis, were requisitioned by direct authority of the President of the United States: the NA-69s on AEC No. 138 dated February 28, 1941, and the NA-68s on AEC No.140 dated March 4, 1941. Wright Field directed that the NA-50As (as they termed them) be shipped to Sacramento, California, and modified to take U.S. .30-caliber M-2 machine guns "for subsequent assignment to an Air Corps training activity."

Meanwhile, Wright Field notified the Philippine Air Depot by telegram on March 27, 1941, to designate the NA-44s as A-27s, and assigned USAAC serials 41-18890 to 41-18899 to these. The same day, they wired Sacramento Air Depot to designate the NA-50As as P-64s and assign serials 41-19082 to 41-19087. Interestingly, however, Wright Field directed that the first of these (they cited 41-19016, apparently in error) be flown to Wright Field by a Lieutenant Kennedy on May 22, 1941, "for armament installation checks."

Wright Field had to hustle with regard to the new A-27s, but did manage to issue T.O. 01-60HA-2 dated May 1, 1941, an "Airplane and Spare Parts" manual for the A-27, described in subtitles as "Model NA-44 Airplane, Two Place Light Attack-Dive Bomber, Thai."

The A-27s were subsequently assigned to the 4th Composite Group in the Philippines, and contrary to popular belief, saw considerable use there. Here is a summary of the fates of these singularly interesting (and exotic) Air Corps aircraft:

41-18890 Lost in a crash April 21,

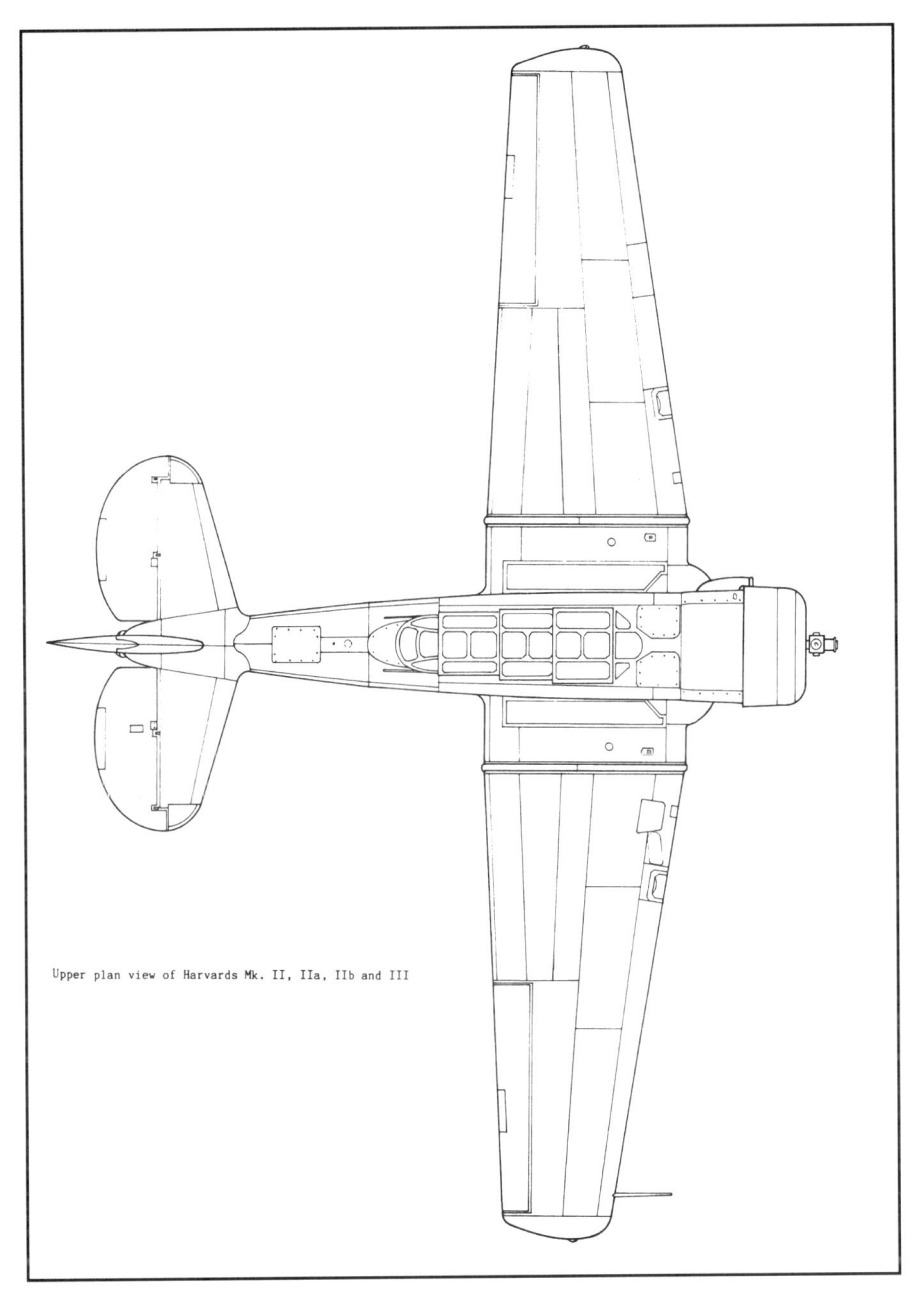

The definitive shape of the Harvard II, IIa, IIb and III and identical U.S. Army Air Force versions in the AT 6, AT 6C and AT-6D series are seldom viewed from overhead. Compare this view with that of the Harvard I to see the evolution of the design. (Courtesy of Air-Britain Historians, Ltd.)

1941, although the pilot used his parachute successfully.

41-18891 Crashed September 17, 1941.

41-18892 Ground looped September 10, 1941, and was apparently still under repair at the time of the Japanese attack.

41-18893 Lost in a mid-air collision on April 21, 1941, (apparently with 41-18890).

41-18894 Condemned November 8, 1942 (a non sequitur meaning it was probably captured by the Japanese, intact).

41-18895 Same as 41-18894.

Unquestionably the most potent variant of the NA-16 family, the six NA-50As built for the Royal Thai Air Force in late 1939 and early 1940 could mount two 20MM cannon and four .30-caliber machine guns, plus bombs racks. (NAA 68-0-7 via Warren M. Bodie and David W. Ostrowski)

41-18896 Wrecked September 10, 1941, when the pilot attempted to take off with the prop in high pitch.

41-18897 Wrecked May 21, 1941, repaired and fate as 41-18894.

41-18898 Same as 41-18894.

41-18899 Same as 41-18894.

Thus, it would appear that of the 10, half survived intact through December 7, 1941, and probably engaged in some form of flying activity, although there are no known instances of combat activity.

NA-71

NAA Designation: NA-16-3
NAA Charge Number: NA-71
Mfg. S/N: 71-3074 to 71-3076
User Regn. or S/N: X-19973 and FAV 1 to 3

The six NA-50As for Thailand never left the United States; they were procured through a direct Presidential order for the U.S. Army Air Corps. This view shows the Thai camouflage and national insignia placement to good advantage, as well as the NA-16 heritage. (NAA 68-0-9 via H. G. Martin and David W. Ostrowski)

Venezuela, happy with the earlier trio of NA-45s placed a follow-on order for three NA-71 General Purpose Combat Airplanes (described in other NAA documents as "ground cooperation aircraft") on January 18, 1940. These were completed and shipped by surface means to Caracas in early July 1940.

The first of these was issued U.S. Identified (Experimental) Aircraft Number X19973 circa May 1940, apparently for flight tests, before delivery, a fact seldom reported. The NA-71s had 550HP Pratt & Whitney R-1340-S3H1 Wasp engines. All three survived in service as late as September 1942 and probably later. They had two .30-caliber guns over the nose (synchronized) and a flexible rear gun, but no wing guns. Bomb racks were available under the mid-fuselage centerline.

NA-72

NAA Designation: NA-44 (BC-1A)
NAA Charge Number: NA-72
Mfg. S/N: 72-3077 to 72-3096; 72-4757 to 74-4766
User Regn. or S/N: Brazilian Army 01 to 30

Ordered in two batches of 20 and 10 each (increased on August 7 1939), the order for 30 NA-44 Light Attack Bombers for the Brazilian Army was a direct result of the earlier demonstrations made by the 'original' NA-44, NX-18981, although the aircraft flight-delivered to Brazil had little in common with the original.

The Brazilian aircraft made Western Hemispheric aviation history when, commencing on October 13, 1940, the first six of these aircraft landed at Rio de Janeiro after a 10,000 mile, trail-blazing delivery flight, the first such flight of such length. The remaining aircraft were also flight delivered, usually in groups of six, with the last examples arriving in February 1941. The route chosen took the aircraft from Inglewood down the Pacific Coast of South America to Santiago, Chile and thence across the Andes to Buenos Aires, in Argentina, and then up the coast to Rio!

NA-74

NAA Designation:	NA-44
NAA Charge Number:	NA-74
Mfg. S/N:	74-4745 to 74-4756
User Regn. or S/N:	Chilean Air Force 1 to 12 later 201 to 212

Not to be outdone by rival South American power Brazil, and possibly influenced by the performance displayed during transit of Brazilian NA-44s through Santiago, Chile placed an order for 12 virtually identical NA-74s (also referred to as "light attack bombers") on August 7, 1940.

Oddly, these aircraft were invariably cited in U.S. intelligence reports as NA-49s, although the Chileans referred to them sometimes (in error) as NA-14s, but usually as NA-44s. One was lost on August 21, 1941, after the May-June delivery, but the remaining 11 survived the war years, and 10 were still on strength as late as January

After being taken by the USAAC and designated as P-64s, the six NA-50As retained the Thai camouflage and only rudimentary U.S. insignia for a time, as Wright Field took a while to assign U.S. serial numbers to the aircraft. (Harold W. Kulick)

Thailand also ordered 10 NA-44 (NA-69) light attack bombers to complement their NA-50As, and these had actually gotten to Manila in the Philippines when the U.S. Presidential order embargoed them in favor of the USAAC. (NAA 69-0-3 via David W. Ostrowski)

Although published once before, this image of two of the Thai NA-44s (NA-69s) taken over by the USAAC and used in the Philippines as A-27s had been printed backwards; this is the correct view. Of the 10 aircraft, four were still airworthy at the time of the Japanese attack. (Fairchild Photo #44-398 via David W. Ostrowski)

NORTH AMERICAN
NA-16/AT-6/SNJ

The Brazilian Army bought 30 NA-44s (NA-72s), which were flight-delivered by Brazilian crews, a direct result of the earlier demonstrations throughout Latin America by NA-44 NX-18981. These aircraft were also light attack aircraft and had a distinguishing ADF 'bullet' under the forward fuselage. (Gustavo Wetsch)

Not to be outdone by rival Latin American power Brazil, Chile also ordered 12 NA-44s (NA-74s) that were virtually identical seven months later, in August 1940. Here, the first aircraft, S/N 201 (C/N 74-4745) reveals the port wing gun blister, bomb rack positions and smaller ADF bullet that were unique to the Chilean aircraft. (Sergio Kreft/FACh)

1946. The Chilean NA-74s mounted three forward-firing guns (one over the nose and one in each wing) and had two A-3 bomb racks under each outer wing panel. A distinguishing recognition feature was a small D/F loop under the forward fuselage, between the wheel wells, a feature also common to the Brazilian NA-72s.

NA-75 (HARVARD Mark II)

NAA Designation: (Harvard Mark II)
NAA Charge Number: NA-75
Mfg. S/N: 75-3048 to 75-3057; 75-3418 to 75-3507
User Regn. or S/N: RCAF 3134 to 3233

An RCAF contract dated June 3, 1940, ordered a follow-on batch of 100 more Harvard Mark IIs, which were identical to the NA-66 series ordered in 1939. These were exclusively intended for the RCAF and were procured on Contract CAN-15.

NA-76 (HARVARD Mark II)

NAA Designation: (Harvard Mark II)
NAA Charge Number: NA-76
Mfg. S/N: 76-3508 to 76-3957
User Regn. or S/N: RAF AJ538 to AJ987

A batch of 450 NA-76s had been ordered by the French, but the country was overrun by the Germans before deliveries could commence. The entire batch was taken over by the British Commonwealth as Harvard IIs. This example, AJ832, spent its entire service life in Canada, first with the Commonwealth 37 SFTS and later with the RCAF. It was photographed at Winnipeg, Manitoba, on July 1, 1947, when it was an RCAF aircraft still bearing RAF insignia and serial. (Leo J. Kohn)

It is not generally understood that this major production batch of 450 aircraft was originally intended for France, but with the events there unfolding faster than deliveries or the means to deliver could be arranged, the contract dated June 5, 1940, was taken over by Britain. Of these aircraft, all but the following were delivered for use in Canada in the CATS:

AJ911 crashed in the United States before delivery.

AJ598 to AJ642; AJ663 to AJ682; AJ703 to AJ722; AJ738 to AJ752 were all delivered for use in Southern Rhodesia.

AJ768 to AJ782; AJ787; AJ803 to AJ822; AJ837 to AJ846 were all assigned to Commonwealth units in the Middle East.

AJ783 to AJ786 were assigned to RAF units in India.

AJ855 to AJ892 were delivered to New Zealand and used there by the RNZAF.

It is not clear what use the French intended, originally, for these aircraft, but it must be assumed that they would have been employed primarily in their training establishment had they been delivered in time.

NA-77 (AT-6A AND SNJ-3)

NAA Designation:	(AT-6A-NA & SNJ-3)
NAA Charge Number:	NA-77
Mfg. S/N:	(see below)
User Regn. or S/N:	

Structural changes in the AT-6A and SNJ-3 series in this joint Army/Navy contract for 517 and 120 aircraft respectively (Air Corps Contract AC-12969 dated June 28, 1940, modified to include the SNJ-3s by Change Order No.8) resulted in the final dimensions of the NA-16 series.

The only technical differences between the two aircraft—a paper exercise at that—were in the designations of the engines: R-1340-49 for the AT-6As and R-1340-38s for the Navy SNJ-3s.

The origins of this Royal Canadian Navy Harvard II, serial 3264, are not known, as the manufacturer's serial number has not surfaced. It was originally taken on charge by the RCAF January 5, 1942, and was transferred to the French Air Force under Canadian aid on October 21, 1957. (Leo J. Kohn)

The breakout of Manufacturer's Serial Numbers to Air Corps and Navy Bureau Numbers for these aircraft was as follows:

AC41-149 to AC41-323 (175 aircraft) were Mfg. S/N 77-3958 to 77-4282 in the same order.

Bu. No. 6755 to 6764 (10 aircraft) were Mfg. S/N 77-4283 to 77-4292 in the same order.

With the distinctive Canadian Harvard II radio mast atop its aft canopy structure and an RDF loop, RCAF 3766 is shown in its June 1953 configuration at Brantford, Ontario. It served during the war with 8 and 14 SFTS, having been taken on charge in April 1941 (MSN 81-4033) and finally stricken on October 18, 1960. (Leo J. Kohn)

A U.S. Navy SNJ-3C about to snag the arrestor hook as it lands onto aircraft carrier (USS Charger) sometime prior to August, 1942. Reportedly, the hooks on the SNJ-3Cs were all second-hand, having formerly been used on Grumman F3F biplane fighters. Note the heavily reinforced and armored tail wheel assembly and hook retainer just ahead of the tail wheel. (National Archives 80G-20106 via Hal Andrews)

AC41-324 to AC41-343 (20 aircraft) were Mfg. S/N 77-4293 to 77-4312 in the same order.

Bu. No. 6765 to 6774 (10 aircraft) were Mfg. S/N 77-4313 to 77-4322 in the same order.

AC41-344 to AC41-373 (30 aircraft) were Mfg. S/N 77-4323 to 77-4352 in the same order.

Bu. No. 6775 to 6784 (10 aircraft) were Mfg. S/N 77-4353 to 77-4362 in the same order.

AC41-374 to AC41-393 (20 aircraft) were Mfg. S/N 77-4363 to 77-4382 in the same order.

Bu. No. 6785 to 6794 (10 aircraft) were Mfg. S/N 77-4383 to 77-4392 in the same order.

AC41-394 to AC41-423 (30 aircraft) were Mfg. S/N 77-4393 to 77-4422 in the same order.

Bu. No. 6795 to 6804 (10 aircraft) were Mfg. S/N 77-4423 to 77-4432 in the same order.

AC41-424 to AC41-443 (20 aircraft) were Mfg. S/N 77-4433 to 77-4452 in the same order.

Bu. No. 6805 to 6814 (10 aircraft) were Mfg. S/N 77-4453 to 77-4462 in the same order.

AC41-444 to AC41-473 (30 aircraft) were Mfg. S/N 77-4463 to 77-4492 in the same order.

Bu. No. 6815 to 6824 (10 aircraft) were Mfg. S/N 77-4493 to 77-4502 in the same order.

AC41-474 to AC41-503 (30 aircraft) were Mfg. S/N 77-4503 to 77-4532 in the same order.

Bu. No. 6825 to 6834 (10 aircraft) were Mfg. S/N 77-4533 to 77-4542 in the same order.

AC41-504 to AC41-543 (40 aircraft) were Mfg. S/N 77-4543 to 77-4582 in the same order.

Proof that pre-war USAAC markings lasted until at least May 30, 1942. Here, at least 29 AT-6As from two different batches adorn the ramp at Napier Field, Alabama. Note that on more than half, the rear gunner's enclosure was retracted or removed entirely. (USAF G 782, National Archives RG 18)

Bu. No. 6835 to 6844 (10 aircraft) were Mfg. S/N 77-4583 to 77-4592 in the same order.

AC41-544 to AC41-583 (40 aircraft) were Mfg. S/N 77-4593 to 77-4632 in the same order.

Bu. No. 6845 to 6854 (10 aircraft) were Mfg. S/N 77-4633 to 77-4642 in the same order.

AC41-584 to AC41-623 (40 aircraft) were Mfg. S/N 77-4643 to 77-4682 in the same order.

Bu. No. 6855 to 6864 (10 aircraft) were Mfg. S/N 77-4683 to 77-4692 in the same order.

AC41-624 to AC41-653 (30 aircraft) were Mfg. S/N 77-4693 to 77-4722 in the same order.

Bu. No. 6865 to 6874 (10 aircraft) were Mfg. S/N 77-4723 to 77-4732 in the same order.

AC41-654 to AC41-665 (12 aircraft) were Mfg. S/N 77-4733 to 77-4744 in the same order.

The first AT-6A was delivered to the Air Corps on September 27, 1940. These 637 aircraft were the last large block of NA-16/AT-6/SNJ aircraft built at Inglewood, and were definitively identified therefore as AT-6A-NAs.

Some of the old bugaboos of the earlier NA-16/BT-9 series resurfaced to plague the AT-6A and SNJ-3s, however, despite vast improvements over the intervening five years. Technical Order 01-60FD-9, dated June 5, 1942, warned that "test spins have proven that it is impossible in some cases to recover from spins in less than four and one-half turns in some AT-6A airplanes." Pending the installation of what was termed a "tripod reinforcement in the vertical stabilizer" AT-6As AC41-149 to 41-785 (and 41-15824 to 41-15883) were prohibited from intentional spinning until the modification was completed.

Also note that AT-6As and SNJ-3s were capable of accommodating only two .30-caliber machine guns: one over the starboard nose, synchronized, and the flexible gun.

NA-78 (AT-6A, SNJ-3 and SNJ-3C)

NAA Designation:	(AT-6A-NT & SNJ-3/C)
NAA Charge Number:	NA-78
Mfg. S/N:	(see below)
User Regn. or S/N:	

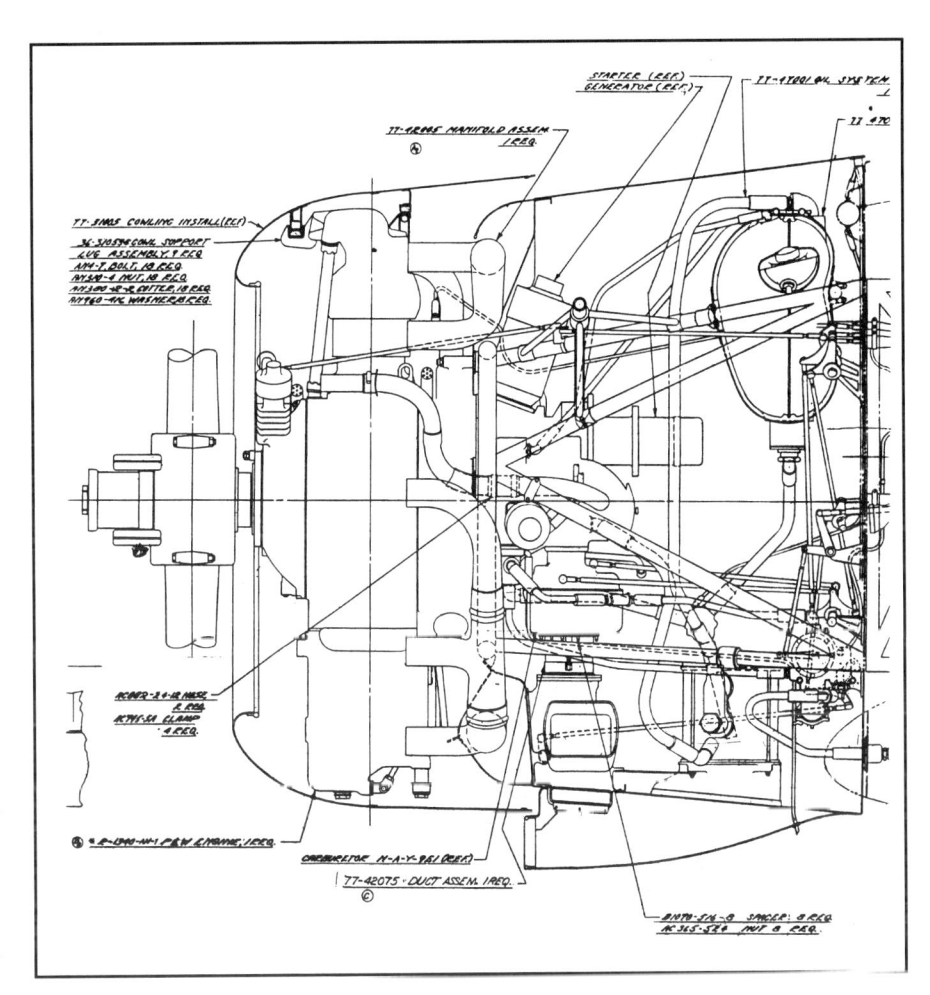

The engine mount assembly and piping for the AT-6A and SNJ-3. (USAF Engineering Drawings on Microfilm, NASM)

Contract AC-12969 was followed by an even larger one on AC-15977, dated October 1, 1940, for not fewer than 1,330 AT-6As for the USAAC and 150 more SNJ-3s for the Navy. Although these totals, shown in the *NAA O Report* were significantly modified before production of the two types terminated: a total of 568 aircraft eventually were changed on the line, under Army orders for the Navy, as SNJ-3s, and 400 were completed as AT-6Bs with the same NAA charge number. Many published sources have considerably confused these offset deliveries and correspondingly the assigned USAAC and U.S. Navy serials.

These aircraft were to be built at the new NAA factory facility near

Nine mixed AT-6A-NTs and AT-6A-NAs from the USAAC Gunnery School at Harlingen, Texas, fly in echelon in October 1942, with a variety of marking styles. The only thing they have in common is the painted engine cowling (probably orange). (USAF 24716AC, National Archives RG 18)

Dallas, Texas. Hitherto, the "popular" name for the AT-6 and SNJ series has not been recorded in these pages. This is because, quite simply, the series did not gain the name until production had started in Texas. Thus, commencing about October 1941, the popular name Texan was born—the result of a competition for selection of the name among the workers at the Dallas plant. Little did those Texans know, at the time, how long-lived some of their handiwork—or the name they chose—would be.

Production of the AT-6A-NTs and corresponding SNJ-3s was as follows, according to NAA records:

AC41-666 to AC41-735 (70 aircraft) were Mfg. S/N 78-5932 to 78-6001 in the same order.

Bu. No. 6875 to 6884 (10 aircraft) were Mfg. S/N 78-6002 to 78-6011 in the same order.

AC41-736 to AC41-755 (20 aircraft) were Mfg. S/N 78-6012 to 78-6031 in the same order.

Bu. No. 6885 to 6894 (10 aircraft) were Mfg. S/N 78-6032 to 78-6041 in the same order.

AC41-756 to AC41-775 (20 aircraft) were Mfg. S/N 78-6042 to 78-6061 in the same order.

Bu. No. 6895 to 6904 (10 aircraft) were Mfg. S/N 78-6062 to 78-6071 in the same order.

AC41-776 to AC41-785 and AC41-15824 to AC41-15833 (20 aircraft) were 78-6072 to 78-6091 in the same order.

Bu. No. 6905 to 6914 (10 aircraft) were Mfg. S/N 78-6092 to 78-6101 in the same order.

AC41-15834 to AC41-15853 (20 aircraft) were Mfg. S/N 78-6102 to 78-6121 in the same order.

Bu. No. 6915 to 6924 (10 aircraft) were Mfg. S/N 78-6122 to 78-6131 in the same order.

AC41-15854 to AC41-15883 (30 aircraft) were Mfg. S/N 78-6132 to 78-6161 in the same order.

Bu. No. 6925 to 6934 (10 aircraft) were Mfg. S/N 78-6162 to 78-6171 in the same order.

The U.S. Navy ordered a total of 270 SNJ-3s (NA-77 and 78) concurrent with the Army's AT-6As, and aside from markings, they were almost identical. On the SNJ-3, however, the tops of the wings (and, in some cases, the horizontal tail surfaces) were painted chrome yellow, while Army AT-6As were bare metal. (via Fred Freeman)

AC41-15884 to 15913 (30 aircraft) were Mfg. S/N 78-6172 to 78-6201 in the same order.

Bu. No. 6935 to 6944 (10 aircraft) were Mfg. S/N 78-6202 to 78-6211 in the same order.

AC41-15914 to AC41-15953 (40 aircraft) were Mfg. S/N 78-6212 to 78-6251 in the same order.

Bu. No. 6945 to 6954 (10 aircraft) were Mfg. S/N 78-6252 to 78-6261 in the same order.

AC41-15954 to AC41-15993 (40 aircraft) were Mfg. S/N 78-6262 to 78-6301 in the same order.

Bu. No. 6955 to 6964 (10 aircraft) were Mfg. S/N 78-6302 to 78-6311 in the same order.

AC41-15994 to AC41-16043 (50 aircraft) were Mfg. S/N 78-6312 to 78-6361 in the same order.

Bu. No. 6965 to 6974 (10 aircraft) were Mfg. S/N 78-6362 to 78-6371 in the same order.

AC41-16044 to AC41-16093 (50 aircraft) were Mfg. S/N 78-6372 to 78-6421 in the same order.

Bu. No. 6975 to 6984 (10 aircraft) were Mfg. S/N 78-6422 to 78-6431 in the same order.

AC41-16094 to AC41-16118 (25 aircraft) were Mfg. S/N 78-6432 to 78-6456 in the same order.

Bu. No. 6985 to 7024 (40 aircraft) were Mfg. S/N 78-6457 to 78-6496 in the same order.

AC41-16119 to AC41-16228 (110 aircraft) were Mfg. S/N 78-6497 to 78-6606 in the same order.

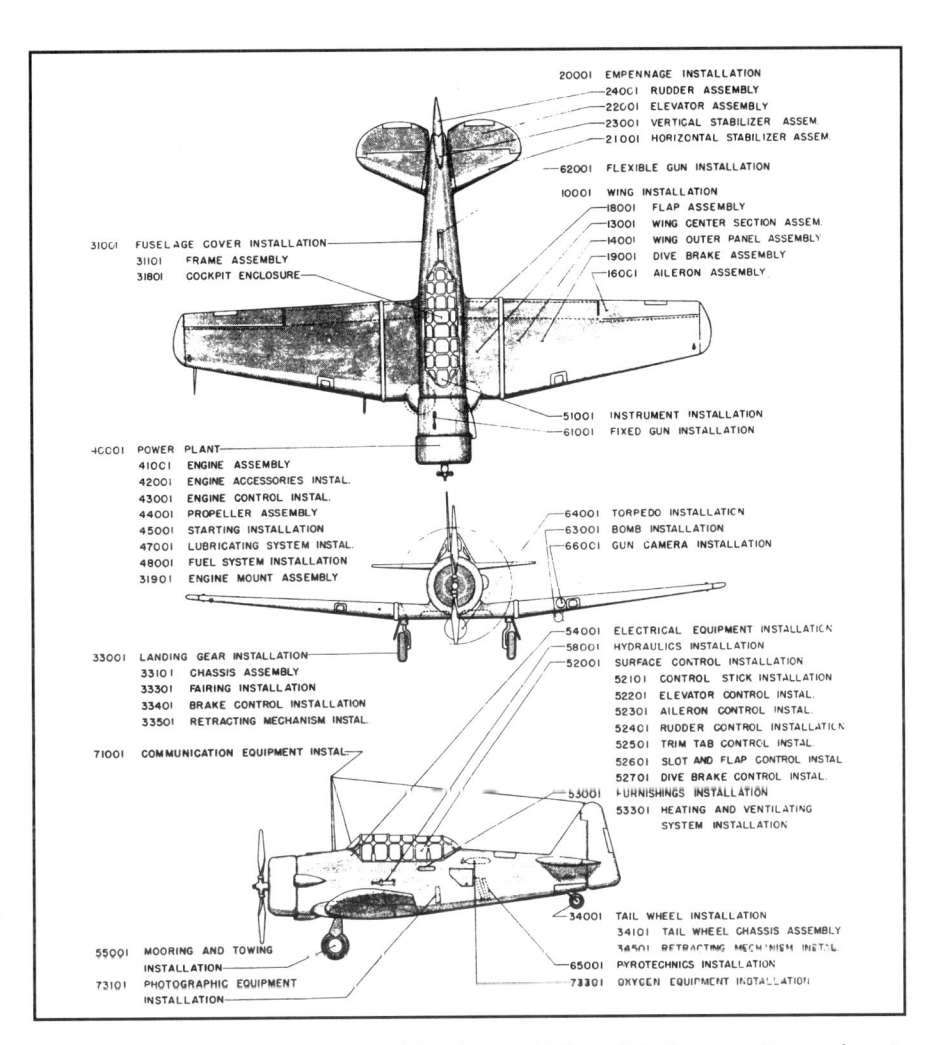

Only 400 NA-84s were acquired by the USAAC as AT-6Bs on a December 6, 1940, contract, and many of them went to Latin America under Lend-Lease. They were dedicated gunnery trainers. This three view illustrates the Parts List for the major components as of November, 1943. Of special note is Part Number 64001, "Torpedo Installation." (T.O. 01-60FE-4)

Bu. No. 01771 to 01800 (30 aircraft) were Mfg. S/N 78-6607 to 78-6636 in the same order (often cited in error as ex-AC41-16229 to 41-16258, these serials were actually canceled).

AC41-16259 to AC41-16403 (145 aircraft) were Mfg. S/N 78-6637 to 78-6781 in the same order.

Bu. No. 01801 to 01835 (35 aircraft) were Mfg. S/N 78-6782 to 78-6816 in the same order (often cited in error as ex-AC41-16404 to 41-16438, these serials were actually canceled).

AC41-16439 to AC41-16457 (19 aircraft) were Mfg. S/N 78-6817 to 78-6835 in the same order.

Bu. No. 01836 to 01851 (16 aircraft) were Mfg. S/N 78-6836 to 78-6851 in the same order (often cited in error as ex-AC41-16458 to 41-16473, these serials were actually canceled).

AC41-16474 to AC41-16578 (105 aircraft) were Mfg. S/N 78-6852 to 78-6956.

Bu. No. 01852 to 01888 (37 aircraft) were Mfg. S/N 78-6957 to

NORTH AMERICAN NA-16/AT-6/SNJ

Britain and Canada ordered another batch of 125 NA-81s on July 11, 1940, designating them Harvard IIs, as they were identical to the earlier NA-66s. Here, RCAF S/N 3782 (C/N 81-4049) is seen in flight after its April 1941 delivery. It served until it was written off in an accident on February 2, 1945. (David W. Ostrowski)

78-6993 in the same order (often cited in error as ex-AC41-16579 to 41-16615, these serials were actually canceled).

AC41-16616 to AC41-16653 (38 aircraft) were Mfg. S/N 78-6994 to 78-7031 in the same order.

Bu. No. 01889 to 01927 (39 aircraft) were Mfg. S/N 78-7032 to 78-7070 in the same order (often cited in error as ex-AC41-16654 to 41-16692, these serials were actually canceled).

AC41-16693 to AC41-16778 (86 aircraft) were Mfg. S/N 78-7071 to 78-7156 in the same order.

Bu. No. 01928 to 01969 (42 aircraft) were Mfg. S/N 78-7157 to 78-7198 in the same order (often cited in error as ex-AC41-16779 to 41-16820, these serials were actually canceled).

AC41-16821 to 16878 (58 aircraft) were Mfg. S/N 78-7199 to 78-7256 in the same order.

Bu. No. 10970 to 10976; 05435 to 05472 (7 and 38 aircraft, respectively) were Mfg. S/N 78-7257 to 78-7301 in the same order (Bu. No. 01970 to 01976 are often cited as ex-AC41-16879 to 41-16885 and Bu. No. 05435 to 05472 are often cited in error as ex-AC41-16886 to 41-16923, but all of these serials were actually canceled).

AC41-16924 to AC41-16979 (56 aircraft) were Mfg. S/N 78-7302 to 78-7357 in the same order.

Bu. No. 05473 to 05526 (54 aircraft) were Mfg. S/N 78-7358 to 78-7411 in the same order (often cited in error as being ex-AC41-16940 to AC41-16993, these USAAC serials were actually canceled).

Some interesting things happened to some of these serial numbers in May 1942, however, that has confounded many historians, and which is being reported here for the first time. Technical Order No. 01-60FC-23, dated May 20, 1942, directed:

"To avoid confusion between the A.C. Serial numbers and the radio call numbers on AT-6A airplanes, AC41-666 to 41-785 inclusive and 41-15824 to 41-16692 inclusive (and AT-6Bs 41-17034 to 41-17111 inclusive) the radio call letters [sic] will be modified in accordance with the following instructions:

a. The first digit in the radio call number will be changed from 2 to 1.

An immaculate AT-6B, USAAF S/N 41-17319 (Radio Call Number 117319, unit number 7), of the South East Air Corps Training Center shows an insignia just visible on its lower fuselage side, as of December 27, 1942. This aircraft was accepted at Dallas on April 29, 1942, and assigned to Valdosta, surviving until December 4, 1945. (USAF 27533AC, National Archives RG18)

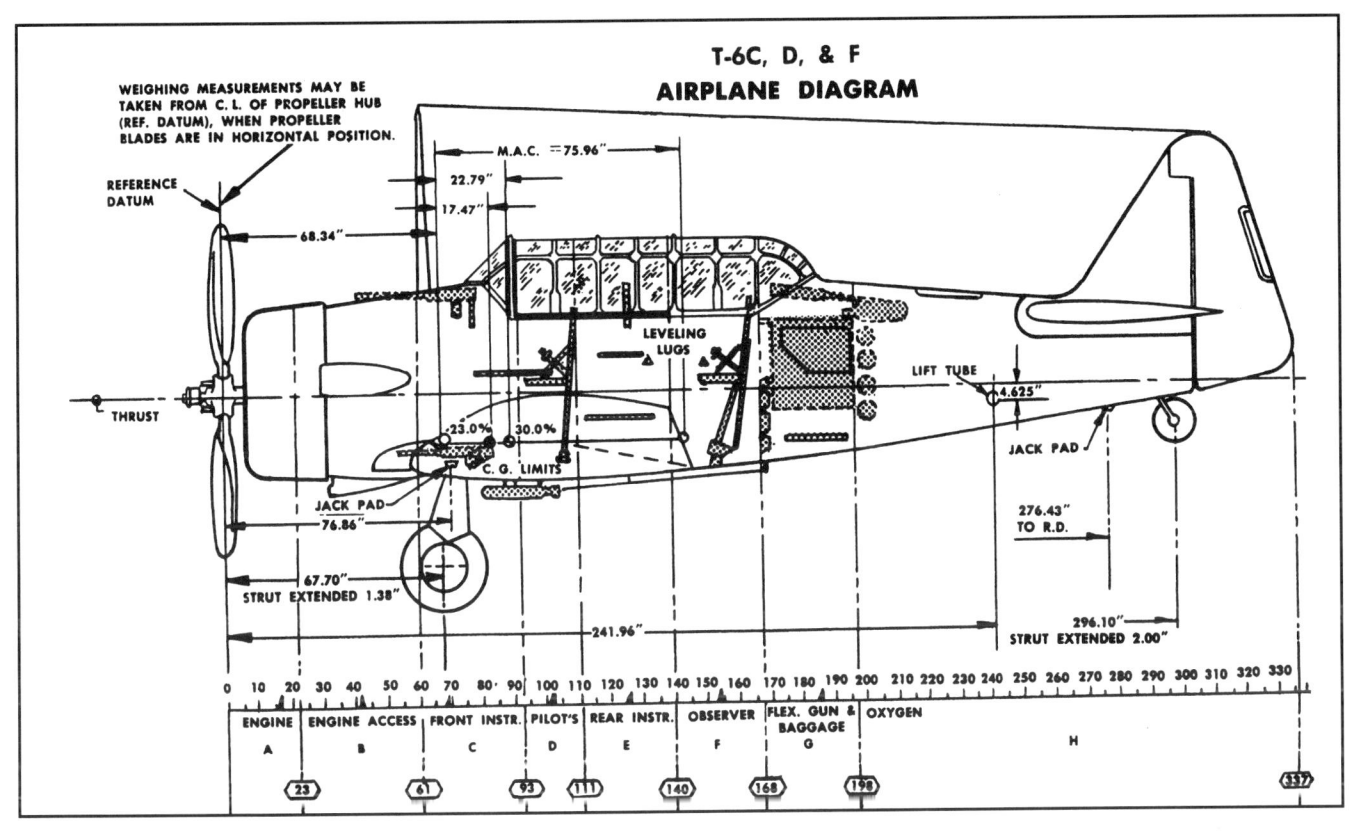

Inboard profile of the post-war T-6C, T-6D and (with some changes) the T-6F series. (T.O. 01-60F-5)

b. The radio call plate on the instrument panel will be replaced with a new call plate bearing the correct number.

c. The radio call numbers appearing on the left-hand side of the fuselage near the tail, in 12 inch block figures, will be modified by removing the first digit and replacing the figure 1."

This may be a convenient point at which to acquaint you with the terminology involved. An aircraft serial number is that which appears (a) on the Manufacturer's Data Plate, along with (usually) the Manufacturer's Serial Number; and (b) on the Data Block painted on the side of most USAAC/USAAF aircraft. The radio call number is the number usually painted on the vertical tail, fin or both and sometimes on the fuselage's sides or rear of USAAC/USAAF aircraft. This radio call number was usually abbreviated by at least one digit. I recommend the fine work by Mr. Dana Bell to help clarify this contentious issue. The net result of this shuffle of radio call numbers is obvious.

The AT-6As were the first aircraft in the series to go to a foreign nation under Lend-Lease. Bolivia acquired three, initially as part of the U.S. Military Mission in that country, as early as December 2, 1941 (AC41-16094 to AC41-16096). Likewise, a significant number of well-worn AT-6As survived World War Two and became cheap, high-time surplus aircraft. Some of these ended up in curious places, including Portugal and at least seven went to Saudi Arabia, including Mfg. S/N 78-6858, NC-252H, in August 1952. AT-6As and SNJ-3s were selling surplus as early as 1947 for $1,450 to $1,875. At least 34 were sold surplus to the Royal Swedish Air Force in 1951 via A.E. Ulman & Associates in New York along with 31 former SNJ-3s and four SNJ-3Cs.

AT-6As and SNJ-3s could mount only two .30-caliber guns—the one over the starboard nose and the flexible gun—with no provisions for bomb racks.

Before leaving these pivotal aircraft, it must be noted that at least 12 SNJ-3s (one source states 55, but this cannot be substantiated) were converted for carrier deck landing training with arrester gear. They were the first Texan series aircraft to perform this vital duty and were thus designated SNJ-3Cs. They included Bu. No. 6792, 6797, 6802, 6854, 6916, 6957 and 7001.

AT-6As that survived in USAAF service into 1948, of which there were a number, were redesignated at that time as T-6A-NTs.

NORTH AMERICAN
NA-16/AT-6/SNJ

Six AT-6C-NTs (NA-88) with 1942 U.S. national insignia and distinctive cowling markings fly in step-down echelon. (David W. Ostrowski)

were given the same name with different Marks. The aircraft with RAF serials were used by SFTSs in Canada, and those that survived passed on to the RCAF retaining these serial numbers.

NA-84 (AT-6B)

NAA DESIGNATION:	(AT-6B)
NAA CHARGE NUMBER:	NA-78
MFG. S/N:	(78)84-7412 to (78)84-7811
USER REGN. OR S/N:	AC41-17034 to 41-17433

The NAA *O Report* originally listed these 400 AT-6Bs, which were acquired for the USAAC as armament trainers, as in the NA-78 (AT-6A/SNJ-2) Charge Number block, which was indeed correct. However, these aircraft were later charged instead against NA-84, due to the significant changes. These aircraft had the R-1340-AN-1 engine of 600HP, a standard .30-caliber dorsal gun with a similar *(text continued on page 69)*

NA-79 (SNJ-2)

NAA DESIGNATION:	(SNJ-2)
NAA CHARGE NUMBER:	NA-79
MFG. S/N:	78-3983 to 78-4007
USER REGN. OR S/N:	Bu. No. 2548 to 2572

Oddly, the contract for the second batch of 25 SNJ-2s, dated June 24, 1940, for the U.S. Navy was let before that for the NA-77s and NA-78s (AT-6As and SNJ-3s), as would seem logical, but because of the nature of the joint Army/Navy production run on these, the SNJ-2s received the next NAA Charge Number in sequence! The Manufacturer's Serial Numbers are much "lower" than the initial AT-6A and SNJ-3 issues.

Be that as it may, however, and even though the SNJ-2s were essentially the same as the British NA-66s (Harvard Mark IIs), they were also acquired on an Army contract (AC-12969, Change #7), but exclusively for Navy use. The SNJ-2s were the last Navy variants built at Inglewood. They mounted the Wright R-1340-56 engine and had a longer wing span than the previous SNJ-1s (up to 42'7").

NA-81 (HARVARD Mark II)

NAA DESIGNATION:	(Harvard Mark II)
NAA CHARGE NUMBER:	NA-81
MFG. S/N:	81-4008 to 81-4132
USER REGN. OR S/N:	RCAF 3014 to 3033; RCAF 3761 to 3841; RAF BW184 to BW207

Yet another follow-on order for 125 Harvard Mark IIs, these aircraft were identical to the previous NA-66s, and were the final "pure" Harvards. All subsequent aircraft with this name produced during the war years were Lend-Lease AT-6Cs and AT-6Ds, and a few ex-USN SNJs

Many AT-6s survived the demands of the wartime training establishment. This AT-6C-10-NT, S/N 42-44055 had only recently gained one of the new buzz numbers (TA-055) when photographed at Milwaukee, Wisconsin, on May 3, 1947. It was reborn later as a T-6G. (Leo J. Kohn)

64

WARBIRDTECH
SERIES

A WORLD OF COLOR

THE TEXAN SERIES PROVIDES INFINITE COLOR AND MARKING VARIATIONS

The NA-16, AT-6, SNJ and Harvard series offer a lifetime's study of color and marking possibilities, and such a study could easily fill several large volumes.

The pre-World War Two Army Air Corps and U.S. Navy variants are fairly well-documented. In particular, the excellent Air Force Colors series by Dana Bell (Squadron/Signal) is an invaluable guide to the standard Air Corps colors. Similar studies of Navy and Marine Corps aircraft have been done, but in a more piecemeal fashion, requiring rather more research.

The export versions built by NAA were painted (or not) and marked per the specifications of the customers, and unfortunately details of the colors used have apparently not survived. Invariably, it appears that most, if not all, of these aircraft received additional markings upon reaching their service destination, some quite colorful, such as the Brazilian Navy NA-46's colors.

This AT-6A-NT, S/N 41-16093, was being used as a gunnery trainer, and still bears the "Army" logo under the port wing and 'Field Number' Z-410. (USAAC via David W. Ostrowski)

These two AT-6C-10-NT aircraft, with S/N 42-43925 the nearest, feature olive drab cowlings and "Field Numbers" X-151 and X-152 in this 1942 view. U.S. training bases had their own unique number identifying system for each base. (USAAC via David W. Ostrowski)

NORTH AMERICAN
NA-16/AT-6/SNJ

Even the post-war survivors saw an enormous variation in markings, especially in foreign use. The Squadron/Signal "In Action" number on the T-6 is an excellent source for details on these, but countless more examples await documentation.

Post-war war bird and rebuilt T-6s have suffered greviously at the hands of some owners, and have in many instances enjoyed rather poor attention to detail. Some few are truly excellent. Most recently, I

The second SNJ-2 ever built, U.S. Navy Bureau Number 2009, is shown in the wonderful pre-WW2 Navy colors of the period. It is being flown by Commander Don F. Smith, USN, and 1st Class Machinist Mate Harold Dietz enjoys the ride in the rear cockpit. This aircraft was accepted by the Navy April 22, 1940, survived the war, and was stricken on April 30, 1946. (Rudy Arnold Collection C-237, NASM)

A camouflaged T-6C (FAD 1040) of the Dominican Air Force in November 1972. The radio mast had been added by the U.S. civilian source. (Rafael Power)

Yet another, more modern radio mast adorns this T-6C/SNJ-4, FAH 202, of the Honduran Air Force, which has since been sold into the U.S. as N2781P. (Bob Haney)

saw a T-6 racer named *Lickety Split*, which surely deserves a modeling attempt and must be seen to be truly appreciated.

Besides the technical aspects of the T-6 series presented herein, I attempted to show a wide range of colors and marking detail on every variant, but the color selection is, unfortunately, only a tiny fraction of the amazing breadth of possibilities.

The pre-WW2 USAAC trainer color scheme was truly memorable, as evidenced by this beautiful in-flight view of a BT-9A. (via David W. Ostrowski)

Another view of LT-6G S/N 49-3594 in Korea in 1952 while assigned to the 6147th TCG. (via Robert F. Dorr)

Shown is an LT-6G in Korea while assigned to the 6147th TCG in 1952. S/N 49-3594 passed to the South Korean Air Force under MDA in April 1957. (via Robert F. Dorr)

NORTH AMERICAN
NA-16/AT-6/SNJ

Wings await matching to SNJ-3 and AT-6B aircraft at the NAA factory in 1942. Included in this view are Chilean, USAAC, U.S. Navy, RAF and Brazilian insignia. (NAA via Tom A. Fort, Heritage Museum of South Texas)

This Paraguayan Air Force AT-6D is actually a former Brazilian Air Force Lend-Lease aircraft that was seconded to Paraguay by Brazil in 1960. It was photographed in January 1972 at Asuncion. (George Von Roitberg)

One of the last surviving T-6Gs of the Ecuadorean Air Force, marked simply as 'CTA,' was photographed at the FAE Mechanics School at Mariscal Sucre Airport in August 1996. (Kolin Campbell)

(text continued from page 64) weapon over the right nose cowl and in the right wing, as well as light bomb rack capability.

The first aircraft (41-17034) was delivered to Wright Field on January 12, 1942, and unit cost of the AT-6Bs was $20,869. The next four went to the Uruguayan Air Force in February 1942. At least 50 of these aircraft were flight-delivered to seven Latin American nations by Presidential Order in early 1942. Like some AT-6As, the Radio Call Letters of AT-6Bs with the serial numbers 41-17034 to 41-17111 were altered per T.O. 01-60FC-23 of May 1942, resulting in a number of recognition problems.

One aircraft (41-17136) was assigned briefly to Wright Field's Bombardment Branch at some point during the war. It was used as the test bed for the mock-up installation of a retractable pilot's armor hood. Another, 41-17034 (the first AT-6B), was also at Wright Field in February 1943 at the Prop Lab being used to test laminated wooden prop blades!

Post-war, AT-6Bs were highly sought after by small air forces due to their built-in weapons capability, and surplus examples were going for around $2,395 to $2,875 in 1947. Many nations acquired small lots, including the Royal Swedish Air Force, which bought at least nine between 1951 and 1953.

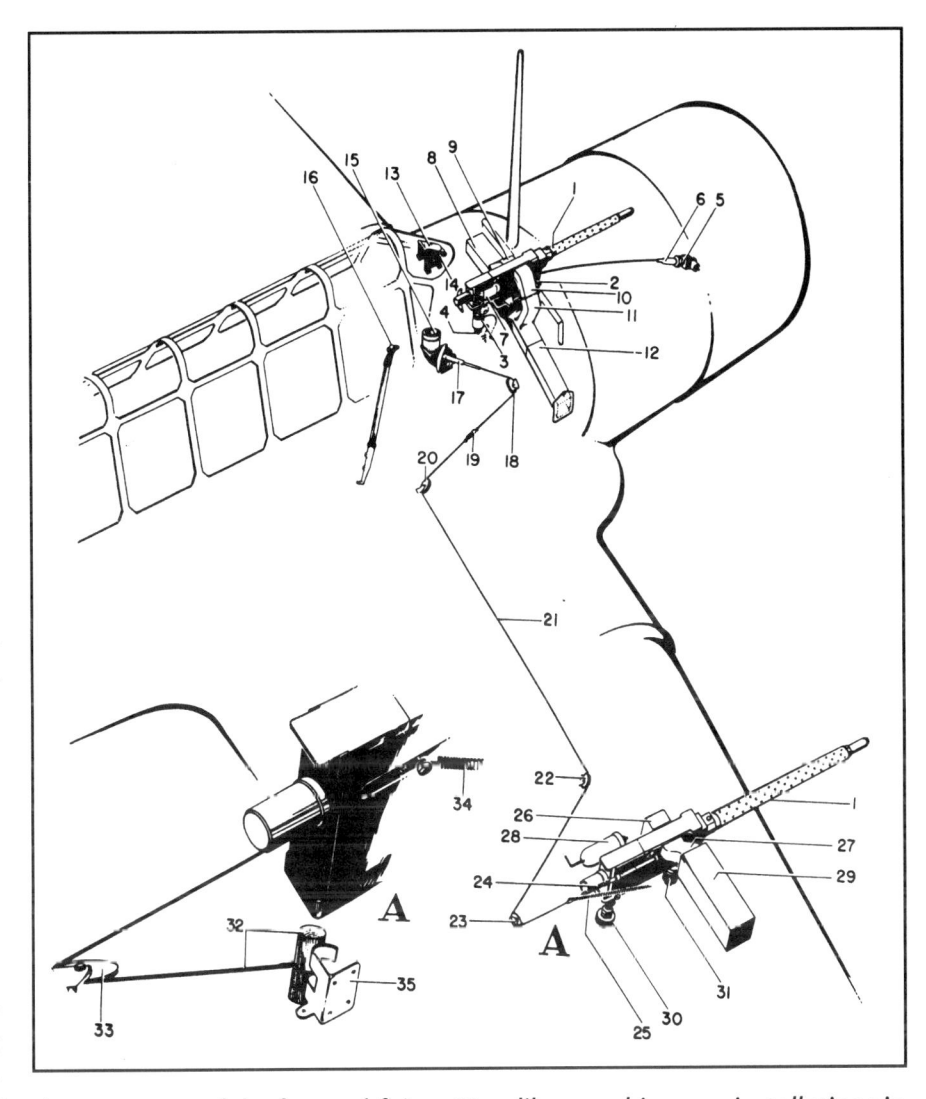

Arrangement of the forward-firing .30-caliber machine gun installations in the AT-6C and SNJ-4. (T.O. 01-60FE-4)

NA-85 (SNJ-3)

NAA Designation:	(None)
NAA Charge Number:	NA-85
Mfg. S/N:	—
User Regn. or S/N:	—

This Charge Number was initially allotted to the 150 SNJ-3s acquired on behalf of the Navy by the Army, but it was eventually included with the NA-78 total order before production commenced.

NA-88 (AT-6C, AT-6D, XAT-6E, SNJ-4 AND SNJ-5)

NAA Designation:	(none)
NAA Charge Number:	NA-88
Mfg. S/N:	—
User Regn. or S/N:	(see below)

This was the major production block of Texan wartime variants. All produced at the Texas plant, these 9,331 aircraft were acquired under four separate contracts: AC-19192, covering 2,970 AT-6Cs; AC-29317, covering 2,604 AT-6Ds (for the USAAF); DA-8, covering 2,401 SNJ-4s; and DA-2799, covering 1,357 SNJ-5s (for the Navy).

The first AT-6C (41-32073) was accepted February 12, 1942, and was assigned for most of its USAAC/USAAF career to Selma Field, Alabama. Incredibly, it survived the war and was supplied to Turkey under the U.S. Defense Aid Program in March 1948.

The AT-6Ds (and later variants) used 24-volt electrical systems, instead

Surviving aircraft were redesignated as T-6s in 1948, and these two aircraft are thus T-6C-15-NTs. The radio mast, gun fairing over the nose, and absence of any apparatus on the upper rear fuselage was usually a tip that the aircraft was a T-6C by this point. (David W. Ostrowski)

of the earlier 12-volt systems, one of the principal differences. The AT-6Cs were almost identical to the AT-6Bs, but made extensive use of low-alloy steel and plywood to conserve scarce aluminum for combatant types at that juncture of the war. This similarity included gunnery capability, although few USAAF aircraft ever mounted guns, while virtually all of those that went to Latin America did.

AT-6C production blocks were as follows *:

AT-6C-NT (963 aircraft) serials 41-32073 to 41-33035.

AT-6C-1-NT (759 aircraft) serials 41-33036 to 41-33794.

AT-6C-5-NT (25 aircraft) serials 41-33795 to 41-33819. (160 aircraft) serials 42-3884 to 42-4043.

AT-6C-10-NT (200 aircraft) serials 42-4044 to 42-4243. (223 aircraft) serials 42-43847 to 42-44069.

AT-6C-15-NT (342 aircraft) serials 42-44070 to 42-44411. (298 aircraft) serials 42-48772 to 42-49069.

[* NOTE: While the Manufacturer's Serial Numbers for all of these blocks are known, they are very complex, and would occupy too much space to reproduce here.]

The last 160 of the AT-6C-5s were fitted with wooden horizontal stabilizers, as were 270 of the SNJ-4s, all of the 443 AT-6C-10s and 640 AT-6D-15s. They also had molded plywood rear fuselage sections in addition to the wooden tails, a detail matched by 1,040 of the SNJ 4s. Many of these were later upgraded to conventional aluminum components during retrofits, especially those supplied to foreign governments under U.S. aid programs post-war. At this time, the AT-6C and AT-6D production was concurrent at the Texas factory well into 1943, a rather strange production anomaly that was due mainly with production for Lend-Lease accounts that were previously obligated to a specific contract and type.

Of this total of 2,970 aircraft, 747 (41-33073 to 41-33819) went to the RAF under Lend-Lease as Harvard IIa aircraft with RAF serials EX100 to EX846. Most of these went to South Africa (436) and the Middle East (100) in October 1942. In December, others went to New Zealand (53) although these were not formally turned over to the RNZAF with their own serials until September 1946, and others went to Southern Rhodesia in January 1943 (149). The histories of these aircraft are clouded by the fact that the South African Air force immediately assigned their own serial numbers to their aircraft (SAAF 7001 upwards). Other minor deliveries were made to British West African bases and to the Royal Navy in India and Ceylon but not a solitary Harvard IIa saw service in the UK itself during the war.

Many of the aircraft in Rhodesia survived the war, and 11 were sold post-war to the Southern Rhodesian Air Force, while some 'struck off' aircraft saw service later in the Belgian Congo with the Belgian Air Force! Post-war, 176 of the SAAF aircraft regained their RAF serials and were shipped back to the United Kingdom. Of these, a significant number were sold to foreign air forces, accounting for the proliferation of Harvards seemingly everywhere after the war. Twelve others were sold to the Dutch directly from South Africa for use as spare parts sources, while many others continued in service with the SAAF up through the present moment.

The British Commonwealth disposition of Lend-Lease Harvard IIa aircraft was a matter of considerable contention on the joint U.S/British Munitions Control Board. On December 11, 1945, the Board

CORRELATED SERIAL NUMBER CHART

Model	NAA Sequence Numbers	Contract	British Serial Nos.	AAF Serial Numbers	Navy Serial Numbers
AT-6D	5371 thru 5372	88	EX847 thru EX848	42-44412 thru 42-44451	51677 thru 51726
AT-6D	5373 thru 5412	88			
AT-6D	5413 thru 5462	88			
AT-6D	5463 thru 5482	88	EX849 thru EX868	42-44452 thru 42-44471	51727 thru 51751
AT-6D	5483 thru 5502	88			
AT-6D	5503 thru 5527	88			
AT-6D	5528 thru 5547	88	EX869 thru EX888	42-44472 thru 42-44517	51752 thru 51801
AT-6D	5548 thru 5593	88			
AT-6D	5594 thru 5643	88			
AT-6D	5644 thru 5663	88	EX889 thru EX908	42-44518 thru 42-44537	51802 thru 51821
AT-6D	5664 thru 5683	88			
AT-6D	5684 thru 5703	88			
AT-6D	5704 thru 5719	88	EX909 thru EX924	42-44538 thru 42-44605	51822 thru 51846
AT-6D	5720 thru 5787	88			
AT-6D	5788 thru 5812	88		42-44606 thru 42-44625	51847 thru 51871
AT-6D	5813 thru 5832	88			
AT-6D	5833 thru 5857	88			
AT-6D	5858 thru 5877	88	EX925 thru EX944	42-44626 thru 42-44645	51872 thru 51896
AT-6D	5878 thru 5897	88			
AT-6D	5898 thru 5922	88			
AT-6D	5923 thru 5947	88	EX945 thru EX969	42-44646 thru 42-44685	51897 thru 51946
AT-6D	5948 thru 5987	88			
AT-6D	5988 thru 6037	88			
AT-6D	6038 thru 6057	88	EX970 thru EX989	42-44686 thru 42-44705	51947 thru 51971
AT-6D	6058 thru 6077	88			
AT-6D	6078 thru 6102	88			
AT-6D	6103 thru 6112	88	EX990 thru EX999		
AT-6D	6113 thru 6127	88	EZ100 thru EZ114	42-44706 thru 42-44725	51972 thru 52021
AT-6D	6128 thru 6147	88			
AT-6D	6148 thru 6197	88			
AT-6D	6198 thru 6218	88		42-44726 thru 42-44746	
AT-6D	6219 thru 6222	88		41-34123 thru 41-34126	52022 thru 52046
AT-6D	6223 thru 6247	88			
AT-6D	6248 thru 6267	88	EZ115 thru EZ134		
AT-6D	6268 thru 6287	88		41-34127 thru 41-34146	52047 thru 52049
AT-6D	6288 thru 6290	88			

This is the official "Correlated Serial Number Chart" for all AT-6D (NA-88 and NA-121) and AT-6F aircraft. (T.O. AN 01-60FF-4)

ruled, "the United Kingdom shall be permitted to continue to use 1,350 *AT-6s* [emphasis author's] as well as 200 B-24s mentioned in COM/Lease 15 for military purposes solely. The U.K. shall not use the 200 B-24s for revenue producing purposes. *Title to the AT-6 and B-24 aircraft shall remain in the United States* [emphasis author's] and the U.K. Government shall offer to return these aircraft when they become excess to U.K. military requirements. U.K. received a net total of 2,693 Harvard IIA, IIB, III (AT-6, AT-16) aircraft at an average of $26,000 each, of which 423 had been lost to attrition by August 30, 1945, and 2,020 remained serviceable."

This is a most interesting passage, especially in view of the fact that the actual numbers of Harvard IIA, IIB and III exceeded 3,841 aircraft, and the U.K. apparently all but ignored the title provisions of the Lend-Lease agreement in its post-war dispositions. This may have been covered by some blanket diplomatic settlement of the U.K. Lend-Lease account, but I have not uncovered such language.

Post-war users of ex-British serialed Harvard IIa, aircraft were as follows:

Belgian Air Force (61) Most were ex-South African, but 24 were from former Southern Rhodesian RAF surplus stocks.

Congolese Air Force (3).

Italian Air Force (13).

Portuguese Air Force (73) of which 59 were ex-South African, 14 ex-Belgian.

Royal Danish Air Force (3) as Instructional Airframes.

Royal Hellenic (Greek) Air Force (35).

Royal Netherlands Air Force (13).

Royal New Zealand Air Force (52).

South African Air Force (as noted).

Factory new from the largest single block of Texans built, 42-85176 was one of 2,400 AT-6D-NTs built in Dallas. It was accepted on June 24, 1944. The position of the individual Radio Call Number is of note. Its first assignment was at West Point. (NAA via David W. Ostrowski)

Southern Rhodesian Air Force (9).

These aircraft were delivered against USAAF orders and actually had assigned USAAF serials, including Individual Aircraft History Cards for each, most of which simply showed the delivery dates and the immediate hand-over to "British Commonwealth" under Lend-Lease.

Another 191 AT-6Cs were transferred under Lend-Lease during the war to various Latin American nations. Post-war, T-6Cs were distributed in significant numbers to many foreign nations under U.S. aid programs, and many others were acquired via surplus dealers.

Besides the low-alloy steel and plywood used in these aircraft, the USAAF also experimented with alternate structural materials. For instance, the AMC contracted with the Virginia Lincoln Corporation, in January 1943 to develop laminated plastic aircraft parts, including rear fuselage sections for AT-6Cs. They used AT-6 40-2080, AT-6A 41-149 (the first AT-6A) and AT-6C 41-32113 for these tests.

Like the AT-6As and AT-6Bs, AT-6Cs suffered confusion with their Radio Call Letters. Ten aircraft arrived at Foster Field, Texas on January 23, 1943, marked on their fuselages as: 42-3989 to 42-3994, 42-3996 to 42-3998 and 42-4019. Their Data Plates, however, read: 41-23989 to 41-23992, 42-23993 to 42-23994, 41-23996, 42-23997, 42-23998 and 42-24019, respectively. Wright Field, to the consternation of Foster Field officers, responded, "the correct numbers are as stamped outside of airplanes."

The U.S. Navy received 2,401 SNJ-4s, which were identical in every respect to the AT-6C. These received Bureau of Aeronautics serials Bu. No. 05527 to 05674; 09817 to 10316; 26427 to 27851, of which 26869 to 27138 had wood stabilizers and 27139 to 27851 had wood fuselage sections. Bu. No. 51350 to 51676 all had wooden stabilizers and rear fuselages. At least 40 of these were converted to SNJ-4Cs for aircraft carrier landing training (the first such was Bu. No. 05587), a function which was extremely hard on the aircraft. A retired naval aviator recalled recently that his class, consisting of approximately 40 aviation cadets, had 18 SNJ-4Cs to use for carrier

Displaying an unusual presentation of the Radio Call Numbers and an odd RDF loop on the upper rear fuselage, 42-85660 was also one of the AT-6D-NTs built in Dallas. It was accepted by the USAAF there on August 16, 1944, and is shown in formation with an odd partner. Intended for Lend-Lease to China, it did not in fact go there, but was sold instead to India in April 1946. (David W. Ostrowski)

training. By the end of the cycle, hardly a single aircraft had escaped some form of damage!

Most accounts of the history of the Texan fail to note that in Fiscal Year 1948 the USAF contracted with North American to essentially rebuild 68 AT-6 variants (including at least 24 ex-USN SNJ-4s) to AT-6C standard. The contract, let before the USAF had changed designation systems, read AT-6C, but in service these were all pure T-6Cs, receiving serials 48-1301 to 48-1368. Incredibly, several returned to the Navy in 1951, presumably as SNJ-4s, but most did not survive training use much beyond September 1952. At least one, 48-1304, went to a USAF school as a training aid. In June 1954, the last known post-war T-6C in USAF service.

The first SNJ-4 (Bu. No. 05527) was accepted by the Navy on May 30, 1942, and not surprisingly, was assigned to Naval Air Station Pensacola. However, it then went to NAS Anacostia for tests, and then back to Pensacola. SNJ-4s could be found virtually everywhere in the Naval Aviation establishment, and training units that used them included VN14D8A, VN14D8B, VN16D8B, VN5D8B, VN6D8, VN2D8A, VN5D8, VTB2, VJ-15 as well as many others, including a number of combat (shore-based) units in the Pacific. One even served as the hack of the U.S. Naval Attache in Colombia (Bu. No. 05500). This was the first SNJ-4 to go overseas when it was assigned to Coco Solo NAS in the Canal Zone.

Post-war, some late production SNJ-4s were surplused with less than 200 hours total time, selling for $2,175 by 1947. The SNJ-4 was also a popular surplus type for foreign military use, mainly due to its comparatively low time in use. Sweden bought at least 27 between 1951 and 1953.

Before leaving the AT-6C and SNJ-4, note that some wartime SNJ-4s did have large yellow upper inner wing panels, reminiscent of pre-war markings, for high-visibility use over water, a key recognition feature.

These huge production runs also included 2,604 AT-6Ds for the USAAF and Allied nations under Lend-Lease, with other AT-6Ds to follow on NAA Charge Numbers NA-119 and NA-121. Conversions to AT-6Fs and post-war cancellations reduced the grand totals of AT-6Ds to 3,958, however, of these, 3,288 were NA-88s. These were produced in the following blocks, which included later add-on batches, and with the USAAF serials noted:

AT-6D-NT (553 aircraft) serials 41-33820 to 41-34372.

AT-6D-1-NT (335 aircraft) serials 42-44412 to 44-44746.

AT-6D-NT (2,400 aircraft) serials 42-84163 to 42-86562.

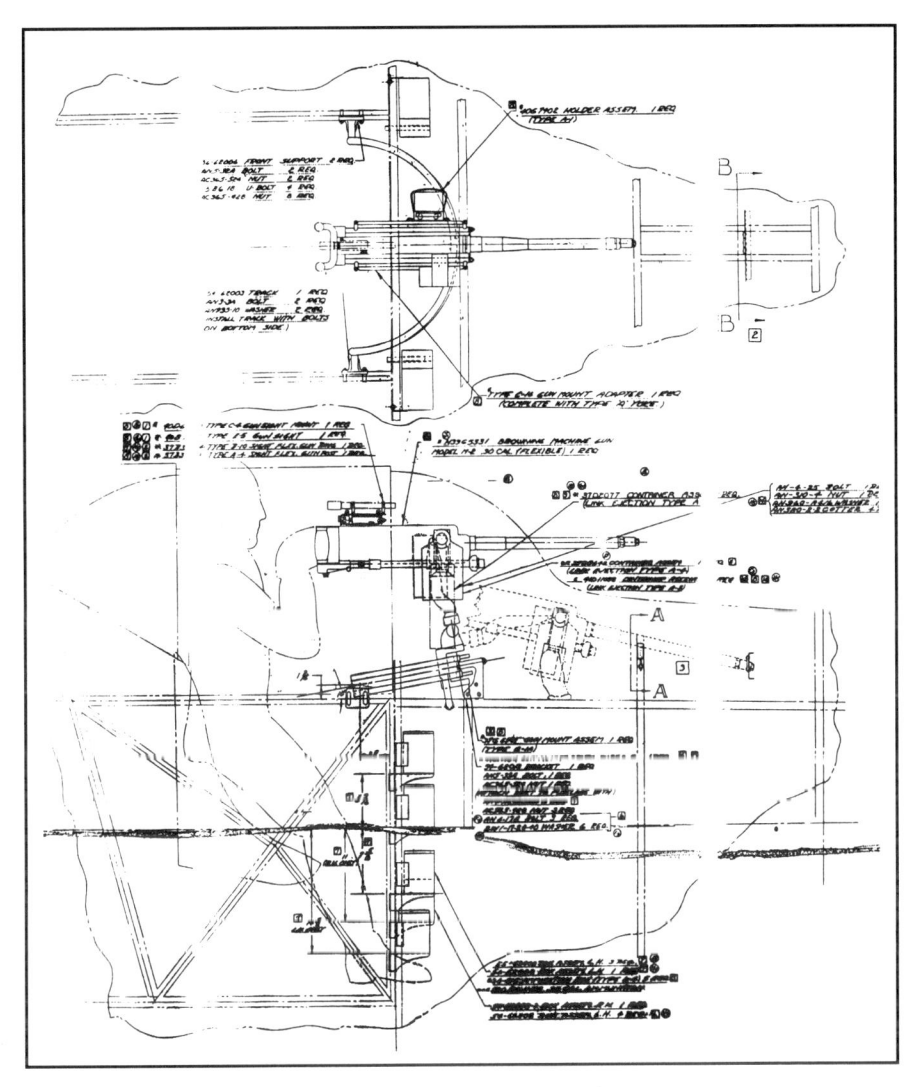

The flexible rear-gun installation was still possible on most AT-6Ds and SNJ-5s, but it was deleted on the AT-6Fs. (NASM)

Nicknames on Texans are not common, but 42-86229R, a T-6D-NT, had been named Flying Jenny *by March 6, 1954, when it was photographed at Milwaukee, Wisconsin. Note the black underbelly of the rear fuselage. The aircraft was probably assigned to a USAF Reserve unit, hence the "R" suffix on the serial.* (Leo J. Kohn)

As noted earlier, the AT-6D was all-metal and certainly one of the most durable of the entire series. It had a 24-volt electrical system, in keeping with a service-wide standardization program. It was also armament capable (although late-production AT-6Ds dropped the rear-gun capability), a feature sought after by Third-World users, but seldom used in USAAF service. The AT-6D series also had flush-type bomb rack capability on the lower surfaces of each outer wing panel, and could mount camera guns. AT-6Ds are distinguishable from earlier variants in having two toggle starter switches in the front cockpit, rather than the foot pedal starter of earlier versions,; an SCR-274N radio; and in late AT-6Ds and SNJ-5s, a demand-type oxygen system. The first AT-6D (41-33820) was accepted July 22, 1943, and was immediately offset to Britain under Lend-Lease. Unit cost for AT-6Ds was $17,992.00, the lowest of the entire series.

Mention must also be made of the solitary XAT-6E, which had been built as AT-6D-NT, S/N 42-84241. It was equipped with a 575HP Ranger V-770-9 engine, in anticipation of a shortage of Wright R-1340 series engines, which never actually materialized. This was an inverted, 12-cylinder engine that achieved almost the same power as the Wright engine from barely half the displacement. The XAT-6E was without doubt the fastest of the AT-6 series, topping out at 244MPH at 22,000 feet, and its service ceiling was 6,000 feet higher than the standard AT-6D. Unfortunately, neither characteristic was necessarily desirable in an advanced trainer, and the V-770 was something of a lemon. The aircraft did survive the war, however, and enjoyed a brief exposure in the 1947 Cleveland National Air Races.

The British Empire received no fewer than 537 AT-6Ds, which they designated Harvard IIIs. These received the following serial blocks:

EX847 to EX999 (153 aircraft) ex-41-33820 to 41-33972.

EZ100 to EZ249 (150 aircraft) ex-41-33972 to 41-34122.

EZ250 to EZ258 (9 aircraft) ex-42-84163 to 42-84171.

EZ259 to EZ278 (20 aircraft) ex-42-84182 to 42-84201.

EZ279 to EZ298 (20 aircraft) ex-42-84282 to 42-84301.

EZ299 to EZ308 (10 aircraft) ex-42-84362 to 42-84371.

EZ309 to EZ328 (20 aircraft) ex-42-84453 to 42-84472.

A considerable number of T-6Ds and T-6Fs saw service in Korea, alongside the better known LT-6Gs. This T-6D-NT, 42-85260A, was photographed at K-16 (Seoul), South Korea, August 28, 1953, and was one of several 6147th Tactical Control Squadron (Airborne) Texans to be fitted with underwing spray tanks to help fight mosquito infestation. The checks on its nose were yellow and black. (Leo J. Kohn)

EZ329 to EZ348 (20 aircraft) ex-42-84543 to 42-84562.

EZ349 to EZ358 (10 aircraft) ex-42-84633 to 42-84642.

EZ359 to EZ378 (20 aircraft) ex-42-84723 to 42-84742.

EZ379 to EZ398 (20 aircraft) ex-42-84803 to 42-84822.

EZ399 to EZ408 (10 aircraft) ex-42-84923 to 42-84932.

EZ409 to EZ428 (20 aircraft) ex-42-85013 to 42-85032.

EZ429 to EZ448 (20 aircraft) ex-42-85103 to 42-85122.

EZ449 to EZ458 (10 aircraft) ex-42-85223 to 42-85232.

EZ459 to EZ799 (allocated to Harvard IIIs but canceled).

FT955 to FT974 (20 aircraft) ex-42-44538 to 42-44557.

KE305 (1 aircraft) ex-USN SNJ-4 Bu. No. 26800.

KE306 (1 aircraft) ex-USN SNJ-4 Bu. No. 26812.

KE307 to KE309 (3 aircraft) ex-USN SNJ-4s Bu. No. 26816 to 26818.

Of the Harvard IIIs, 197 were shipped directly to South Africa between December 1943 and August 1944. One hundred of these returned to the United Kingdom after the war, only one of which was ever actually used in England. Twenty-six others were sold surplus to foreign countries; and 11 remained with the SAAF. Eighty-one went to the Middle East, one of which was turned back over to the USAAF in that region. The EATS in Southern Rhodesia received 70 between December 1943 and July 1944, and 41 went to New Zealand.

The Royal Navy received not fewer than 143 Harvard IIIs. Some of these were returned to the RAF later, but the last Royal Navy (Reserve) example was not retired until 1956. Of the ex-British Harvard IIIs, examples turned up post-war in the following national air forces:

Belgian Air Force (18).

Congolese Air Force (3).

Portuguese Air Force (16).

Royal Danish Air Force (4) As spares and as Instructional Airframes.

Royal Netherlands Air Force (7) Ostensibly for use as spares sources, ex-South African.

Royal New Zealand Air Force (42) Survivors officially transferred to RNZAF ownership in Sept. 1946.

This SNJ-5, Bu .No. 43749, was assigned to NAS St. Louis during 1950, and the crews had apparently decided to ease exhaust stain maintenance. It had been accepted by the Navy on January 27, 1944, and served with various training units, including VN16D8-B and VN5D8-B, until the end of the war. (Ed Ambro via Jim Sullivan and David W. Ostrowski)

South African Air Force (as noted).

You may avoid some confusion if you bear in mind that late in World War Two the British Royal Air Force changed its aircraft designations system from Roman to Arabic figures, and they often added prefixes to these to identify particular missions. For instance, many Harvard II and III series aircraft are often cited as T.Mk.3 and T.T.Mk.3 in the case of those used as target tugs.

At least 219 brand new AT-6Ds were distributed to Latin American nations under Lend-Lease during World War Two, and others went to Nationalist China (at least 20) and the Soviet Union (84). Post-war, T-6Ds were also distributed to a number of foreign nations under U.S. aid programs, prior to the advent of the T-6G series.

The U.S. Navy received 1,987 AT-6Ds, designating them as SNJ-5s. The NAA *O Report* cited only 1,357 SNJ-5s, but did not include subsequent AT-6D offsets to the Navy. It has often been stated that

NORTH AMERICAN
NA-16/AT-6/SNJ

these aircraft had "three machine guns; one dorsal and two wing," but this is not correct. They had the standard complement of three guns: one dorsal, one over the right forward cowl and one in the right wing, when mounted. The SNJ-5s were in the following blocks:

Bu. No. 43638 to 44037 (400 aircraft).

Bu. No. 51677 to 52049 (373 aircraft).

Bu. No. 84189 to 85093 (905 aircraft).

Bu. No. 90582 to 90890 (309 aircraft).

The B suffix is something of a puzzle. Some sources cite an SNJ-5B subvariant, but none have been specifically identified as having been built. The 'B' suffix, in Navy parlance, could mean any one of three things: special modifications, special armament or modification to British Empire standard. So far as can be determined, none of these seem to apply. An unspecified number of SNJ-5s were also converted for carrier landing capability as SNJ-5Cs, but the exact number has not been determined.

ET-6D

At least one post-war T-6D (41-34216) was bailed to North American at Columbus, and it was assigned the designation ET-6D as early as October 1950. Between 1946 and '47, the 'E' prefix indicated an 'Exempt' aircraft, meaning it was not subject to normal change orders, updates, etc., but this prefix was not known to have been used until the 1950s. Nothing more is known about this aircraft, except that it retained this designation until it was reclaimed in April 1954.

AT-16 (NOORDUYN HARVARD IIB)

NAA Designation:	None
NAA Charge Number:	None
Mfg. S/N:	14-1 to 14-800; 14A-801 to 14A-1800
User Regn. or S/N:	(see below)

The AT-16s do not fit neatly into any narrative description of the Texan/Harvard series, as they were actually equivalent, in most respects, to the USAAC AT-6A, and were built completely under license in Canada by the Noorduyn Aircraft Co., Ltd. USAAF documents describe the aircraft as "…designed as a general purpose training aircraft." It differed from most other variants of the Texan/Harvard series in that it mounted only one .303-caliber Browning machine gun, in the right outer wing. It could also accommodate light E.M. bomb racks on either outer wing panel. AT-16s used Pratt & Whitney R-1340-AN-1 Wasp engines and the unit cost was $20,469.00.

Of the total of 2,557 built, 1,800 (usually cited as only 1,500) were paid for under USAAF Lend-Lease funding, which necessitated the AT-16 designation on the Individual Aircraft Record Cards for these. in an exception to the rule, so far as can be determined no NAA Charge Number has been identified for these aircraft. Consequently, these aircraft are often completely overlooked in historical accounts, and several histories of the series do not list them at all.

In addition to the above, two additional blocks of British-funded Harvard IIb aircraft were ordered, but cancelled (KF758 to KF900 and KG100 to KG309, a total of 1,110 aircraft). Fittingly, the Harvard IIbs (nee AT-16) were by far the most numerous in British Empire service. The first examples were completed by Noorduyn in May 1942, and were issued to supplement the

AT-16 (NOORDUYN HARVARD IIB) WERE BUILT IN THE FOLLOWING BATCHES:

USAAF S/N Range	Total	Noorduyn S/N	RAF Serials Range
42-464 to 42-963	500	14-1 to 14-500	FE267 to FE766
42-12254 to 42-12486	233	14-501 to 14-733	FE767 to FE999
42-12487 to 42-12553	67	14-734 to 14-800	FH100 to FH166
43-12502 to 43-12840	339	14A-801 to 14A-1139	FS661 to FS999
43-12841 to 43-13201	361	14A-1140 to 14A-1500	FT100 to FT460
43-34615 to 43-34914	300	14A-1501 to 14A-1800	FX198 to FX497*
(none)	658	14A-1801 to 14A-2458	KF100 to KF757*
(none)	99	18-002 to 18-100	KF901 to KF999

* NOTE: These two blocks are known not to have been in strict numeric order, like the others.

Mark II aircraft that were already serving in the Commonwealth Air Training Scheme. The very first example, however (S/N 42-464), was delivered May 11, 1942, to Wright Field in Ohio, where it spent the rest of the war before finally being surplused at Bush Field in 1946. A notation on its Individual History Card read, "being held for Canada pending contract," but it was apparently never delivered to the RCAF. Deliveries of the remainder to Canadian-based SFTSs continued into December 1943. At that time, 639 had been delivered, but 72 of them were shipped to the United Kingdom in March 1944, some after use in Canada but most after a period of storage. The rate of attrition in Canada was high, but a large number survived to serve on in the RCAF when the RAF elements of the EATS returned home in the fall of 1944.

At least 507 IIbs were shipped to India (to RAF elements), but 17 were lost at sea enroute. Eleven of the aircraft were handed back to the USAAF in October 1943 in India. (So yes, some AT-16s did see USAAF service!) At least 15 additional IIbs were returned to USAAF control in June 1946, and 87 more were scrapped under U.S. Army control. Upon the partition of India, 82 were turned over to the Indian Air Force, 29 to the new Pakistani Air Force, and a further 25 were 'recaptured' by the U.S. Government.

Post-war, Harvard IIbs seemed to turn up everywhere. Known acquisitions were:

Belgian Air Force (31) Of which, 11 were ex-Dutch.

Chinese Nationalist Air Force (200) at least 200, via a broker, post-war.

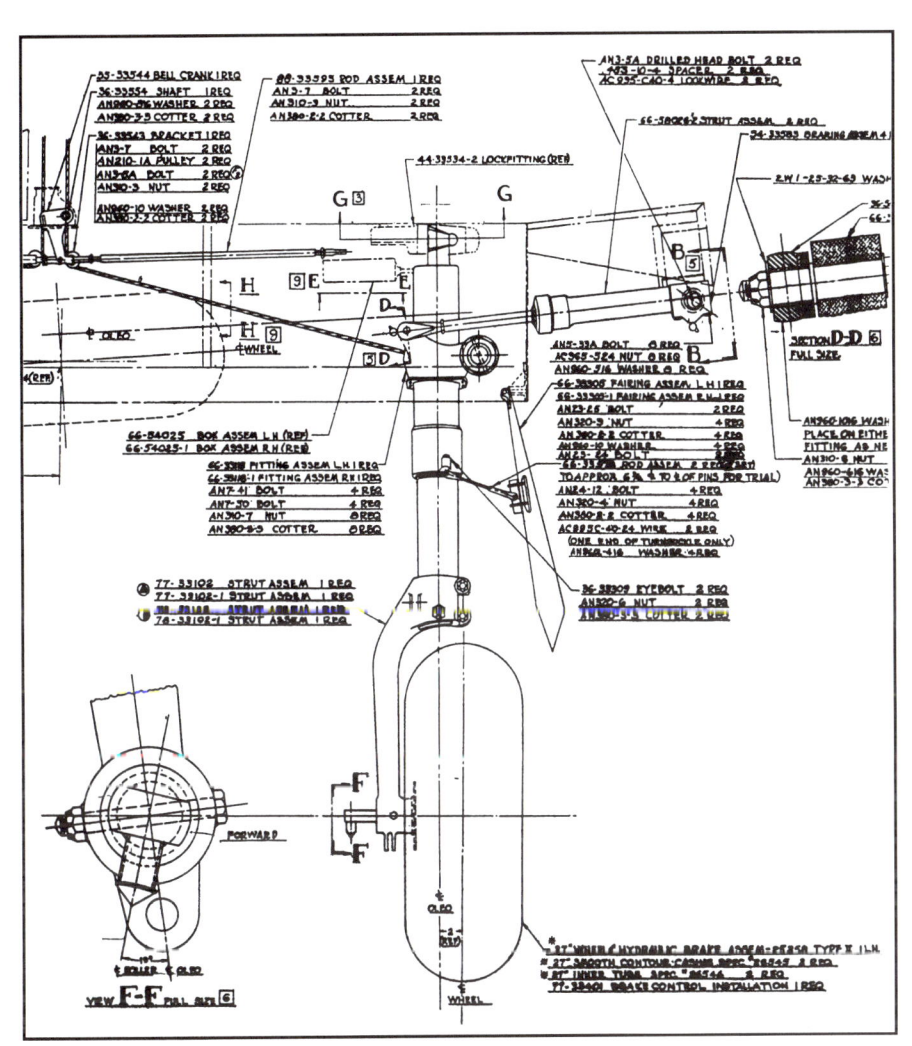

From the earliest retractable landing gear variant of the NA-16 family, there were few changes to the main gear. Shown is a close-up front view of the left main gear on the AT-6D. (NASM)

French Air Force (30) Many of them were never uncrated by the RAF.

Israeli Air Force (1) at least one positively identified.

Royal Jordanian Air Force (3).

Lebanese Air Force (4) At least four and possibly as many as 16.

Royal Dutch Navy (14) On loan from the RNethAF.

Portuguese Air Force (6).

Royal Canadian Air Force (494).

Royal Danish Air Force (31).

Royal Hellenic (Greek) Air Force (30) Of which, 15 had never seen previous use.

Royal Netherlands Air Force (200) Of which, seven were for spares, and at least 155 had never been used before.

Royal New Zealand Air Force (4).

Royal Norwegian Air Force (30) Of which, 23 had been used by the Norwegian Training Base at Winkleigh—Little Norway—in Canada during the war under Lend-Lease.

Noorduyn also built 757 Harvard IIbs, which were not USAAF-procured AT-16s, and KF531 is one example. This aircraft saw post-war service with the RAF (702, 799 and 1834 Squadrons), before it was finally lost in a crash at Ilchester in August 1954. (David W. Ostrowski)

Southern Rhodesian Air Force (11).

Royal Swedish Air Force (144) All ex-RCAF.

Swiss Air Force (2) At least two, ex-RCAF, and probably more.

Syrian Air Force (10).

Turkish Air Force (17) All ex-RNoAF.

Yugoslavian Air Force (10).

The ubiquitous Charles Babb Company purchased not fewer than 491 (some sources say "more than 500") Noorduyn-built AT-16s from the Canadian War Assets Corporation during September 1947, most of which had averaged less than 2,000 hours total time. Of these, at least 75 were sold to Sweden (see above) and at least 200 went to the Chinese Nationalist Government by August 1948. News reports claim that Babb had "sold all of the AT-16s acquired from the Canadian Government" by this time. The destinations of the remainder are not clear, although it is entirely possibly that the remainder were actually sold to North American to serve as the basis for the "postwar T-6D standard" commercial sales effort.

NA-119 (AT-6D FOR BRAZIL)

NAA Designation: (AT-6D)
NAA Charge Number: NA-119
Mfg. S/N: 119-40086 to 119-40166
User Regn. or S/N: FAB 1387 to FAB 1394; FAB 1531 to 1592

Yet another little-known license arrangement was the so-called Brazilian Construcoes Aeronauticas S.A. series of 81 aircraft, funded by the United States under Lend-Lease, Contract AC-1179.

NAA at Dallas shipped 61 complete sets of knock-down components to Brazil, where the CASA workers, the pioneers of today's Brazilian Aerospace industry, learned the hard way about modern construction methods and systems. Ten others were sent as complete airframes sub-assembled, and a further 10 were described as "complete airframes partially subassembled."

These aircraft were not, however, finally accepted by the Brazilian Air Force until February 1946, due to the lengthy on-again/off-again Brazilian Government support for the project and the rather slow progress at the assembly facility. The aircraft were first designated as AT-6Ds in FAB parlance, but later they gained the unusual designation T-6 1LS (the suffix indicates Lagoa Santa, the location of the facility). Some of these aircraft served with the FAB well into the 1970s.

NA-121 (AT-6D, SNJ-5 AND AT-6F, SNJ-6)

NAA Designation: (AT-6D, AT-6F)
NAA Charge Number: NA-121
Mfg. S/N: (see below)
User Regn. or S/N: (see below)

The USAAF originally contracted for 2,175 aircraft under NAA-121, but redesignations and cancellations reduced the total to 589 AT-6Ds, 211 SNJ-5s, which were built as AT-6Ds; and 545 AT-6Fs and 411 SNJ-6s, which were built as AT-6Fs.

These were assigned the following serial number ranges:

AT-6D-NT (800 aircraft) 44-80845 to 44-81644 of which 211 became SNJ-5s.

SNJ-5 (211 aircraft) Bu. No. 90891 to 91101 Built as AT-6Ds.

AT-6F-NT (956 aircraft) 44-81645 to 44-82600 of which 411 became SNJ-6s.

SNJ-6 (411 aircraft) Bu. No. 111949 to 112359 Built as AT-6Fs; an additional 169 ordered as Bu. No. 112360 to 112528 were cancelled.

These aircraft were the final wartime Texans built for the U.S. Armed Forces. In these late AT-6Ds, AT-6Fs and their Navy equivalents, the dorsal/flexible gun provision is eliminated entirely. In fact, the rearmost canopy frame with a fixed, one-piece assembly is a key recognition feature. These aircraft also had considerably strengthened outer wing panels and a provision for a 20-gallon centerline drop tank. The capacity to carry the two standard forward-firing guns was retained. The AT-6Fs and SNJ-6s lost their under-wing, flush bomb rack capability, but retained provision for a gun camera. Many of these late AT-6Ds and AT-6Fs also had prop spinners, the first to appear on any of the NA-16/AT-6/SNJ series. However, many other aircraft were similarly retrofitted post-war, so it must not be used as a positive recognition feature.

Cuba used AT-6Fs, which were delivered under Lend-Lease, the only known foreign offset of new-build AT-6Fs; and the Korean Navy acquired a single aircraft as salvage in late 1950 after a USAF pilot made a forced landing near Kwangji, Korea. This Korean acquisition became the sole NA-16/T-6 floatplane, and apparently actually flew as such in August 1951, after Korean Navy mechanics fitted a single center-line float and F-80 tip-tanks as outboard floats.

Post-war, a number of T-6Fs were supplied to U.S. allies under aid programs. By June 30, 1953, for example, the Royal Thai Air Force was operating 30 MAP-supported T-6Fs, which had been programmed for delivery in June 1951. By 1956, both Japan and Korea were programmed to receive MAP-supplied T-6Fs, and 11 and seven more, respectively, were handed over in the second quarter of that year. Some sources state that a few post-war T-6Fs were remanufactured and designated T-6H-NH. Another well-known source, John M. Andrade's U.S. Military Aircraft Designations and Serials since 1909 (Midland Counties Publications, England, 1979), states that the designation T-6H-CCF was assigned to some of the Canadian Car and Foundry Harvard IVs that were supplied to the Italian Air Force under MSP. However, no documents have been located authenticating the use of this designation.

Never illustrated before, FAB 1387 is one of the 81 AT-6Ds (NA-119s) assembled in Brazil by CASA under a special Lend-Lease arrangement for the Brazilian Air Force. (via George G. J. Kamp)

I must mention one further development of the late AT-6D and AT-6F: A single aircraft, S/N 44-81661, was assigned for duty as a cross-wind landing gear installation test aircraft in December 1, 1950, and it received the designation ET-6F.

NA-128 (AT-6D)

Had the war continued, the 1,200 AT-6Ds on Contract AC-3159 for the USAAF, Navy and Allies on Charge Number 128 would probably have been carried through. However, this last wartime contract for Texans was canceled as the war wound down.

The last wartime AT-6Ds built were 800 AT-6D-NTs (NA-121), such as 44-81354N (a National Guard aircraft) shown here in May 1951 at Milwaukee, Wisconsin. Of special note are the wheel covers and lack of National Guard identity or buzz number. (Leo J. Kohn)

POST-WAR VARIANTS 4

FINAL REFINEMENTS AND A NEW LEASE ON LIFE

The extensive use and world-wide post-war demand that would develop for Texans and Harvards was not immediately apparent to the powers that be. As a consequence, after demobilization the three largest contractors for the series—the United States, Britain and Canada—almost immediately started to dispose of the large numbers of surviving examples, confident that they would surely soon be replaced by the next generation of trainers.

The surplus deluge proved a windfall for arms dealers and brokers of used aircraft, and a still undetermined total of Texans and Harvards of virtually every production variant (including some pre-war examples) quickly found their way into the inventories of Third-World air arms, from Saudi Arabia to Salvador, Spain to Iran.

Although most sources claim that North American did not become aware of this demand until the advent of the T-6G series, this is not correct. The U.S. Government, in particular the early-post war USAF under Hap Arnold, saw in certain World War Two propeller-driven aircraft the means to project the U.S. aviation influence beyond that which had been achieved through Lend-Lease programs and victory.

The little-known Fiscal Year 1948 T-6C conversion of former Navy SNJs and mixed USAAF variants, assigned serials 48-1301 to 48-1368, was performed under Contract AC-19192, which was the same contract under which the original AT-6Cs were built. These 68 aircraft, which were converted by North American at their Inglewood facility in the first T-6 work since early in the war, were the precursors of many T-6D, T-6D Standard and T-6G aircraft, all of which were rebuilds of previous North American products. NAA was, in fact, performing the hat trick of making money twice, and in a number of cases, three times, off the same aircraft.

NAA did not have this field to themselves, however. Although most of the refurbishment and upgrading was accomplished by the company, significant numbers were also worked by TEMCO in Texas and Bellanca in Delaware among others.

The first such T-6D upgrades were 35 Grant Aid T-6D-NTs for the Royal Hellenic (Greek) Air Force that were performed by the NAA plant in Dallas. These aircraft apparently retained their original Manufacturer's Serials and no known NAA Charge Number was assigned to the group, which were assigned serials 49-2722 to 49-2756, a factor that has muddied the waters considerably over the years. The aircraft, like most of the post-war T-6D upgrades, were brought up to late AT-6D standards, nearly that of the AT-6F, but it retained the two forward-firing guns.

Bellanca, at New Castle, Delaware, won a contract from the Air Force to overhaul and modify 30 T-6Ds in October 1949 for the Iranian Air Force under a $250,000 contract. These were delivered in January

SNJ-6s were low-time aircraft at the end of the war, and many passed to Navy Reserve stations, such as Bu. No. 111978 seen at Milwaukee, Wisconsin, on November 28, 1953. The aft canopy section is a key AT-6F/SNJ-6 recognition feature. This aircraft had been accepted by the Navy April 7, 1945, and had served in Hawaii at East Pearl NAS, Kaneohe, NAS Hilo, until returning to Pensacola in 1948. It was then reconditioned there in July 1949. (Leo J. Kohn)

80 WARBIRDTECH SERIES

GENERAL ARRANGEMENT

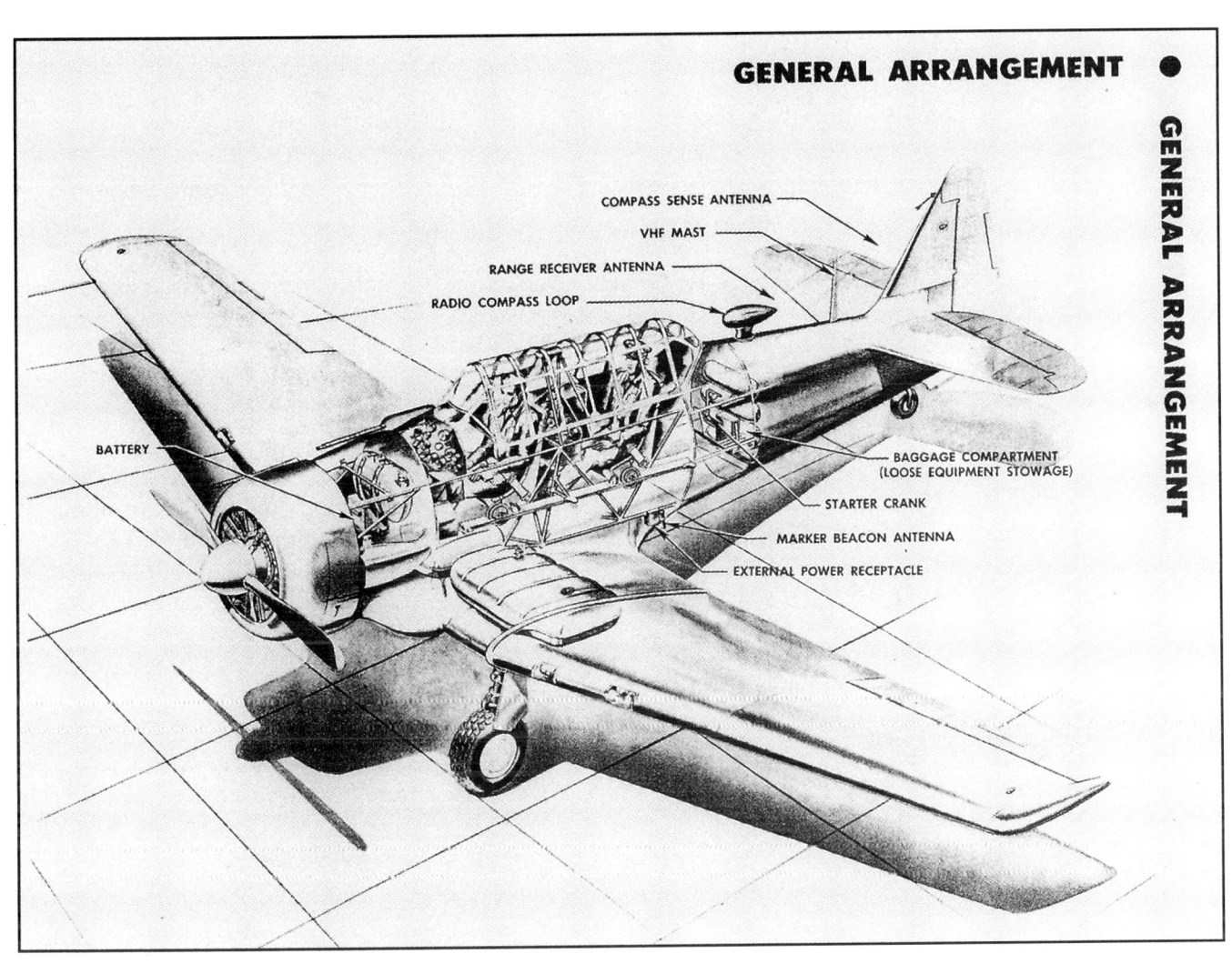

Not to be confused with new-built wartime AT-6D aircraft, during the post-war period and prior to the introduction of the T-6G, NAA and the Air Force brought an unknown number of Texans up to what was often called T-6D Standard. This usually involved the addition of a prop spinner, marker beacon antenna, radio compass loop and VHF radio mast, as shown in this drawing. Note that the two forward guns were retained, as well. (T.O. AN 01-60FFB-1)

and February 1950, and they apparently retained (for accounting purposes) their original AT-6D USAAF serials, not post-war USAF serials. The exact nature of the modifications are unknown.

Similar upgrades continued as the new Mutual Defense Assistance Program (MDAP) evolved. Some of these were performed by contractors, such as TEMCO, which overhauled at least 20 T-6s of an unspecified variant including 10 for Italy in July 1950 and others for the Philippines and Thailand, NAA, Bellanca and A.E. Ulmann & Associates.

Other overhauls consisting mainly of mere Depot level overhauls, were performed by the USAF itself. In still other cases, recipients agreed to accept the aircraft on an "as is/where is" basis and performed the required work themselves. The post-war French Air Force, for instance, received not fewer than 60 T-6Ds under MDAP, while Italy received 30 and Portugal received a mix of variants totaling 20 aircraft. Most, but not all, of these upgraded aircraft could be identified by the addition of a prop spinner, an RDF bullet just aft of the rear cockpit, usually a late AT-6D/AT-6F-style rear solid canopy section, and a smaller radio mast just ahead of the vertical fin. They all retained the wartime style cockpit canopy framing, unlike the later T-6Gs.

Brazil offers a case in point regarding these poorly documented aircraft. In mid-April 1947, under the auspices of the Rio Pact/American Republic Projects, the Brazilian Air Force began to receive not fewer than 100 aircraft, which were identified in transfer documents as "North American AT-6D Standard" aircraft. These received FAB serials

NORTH AMERICAN NA-16/AT-6/SNJ

This Seattle-based SNJ-6, Bu. No.112317, had been painted overall aluminum when it was shot in November 1948. Accepted on July 5, 1945, it originally served with VN16D8-A, and it was stricken in 1948, following a final assignment at Pasadena. (Gordon Williams via Peter M. Bowers)

1397 to 1435 and 1447 to 1506. An examination of the known Manufacturer's Serial Numbers for these 100 aircraft reveals that they included a mix of AT-6A, AT-6B, AT-6C and AT-6D airframes. Some of these were later upgraded locally by the FAB using MAP funds to T-6G Standard. Needless to say, this has added considerably to the confusion over exactly what these aircraft were. The FAB, using its own designation system based on that of the USAF, at different times identified these aircraft as simply AT-6, AT-6D and much later at least 10 were labeled T-6G.

By Fiscal Year 1951, the USAF was supporting the following T-6Ds via the MDAP program worldwide (besides other, unidentified variants):

Belgium (16 aircraft) Delivered by 30 June 1951, in addition to a mix of other variants totaling 82 aircraft.

Denmark (20 aircraft) As of April 1951. One more had been added by June 30, 1953.

Ecuador (7) T-6D Standard aircraft were delivered in the 1st Quarter of FY55.

France (60) A total of 100 T-6D Standard aircraft were programmed for delivery by June 30, 1951, in addition to T-6Gs. However, by June 30, 1953, the total of T-6D Standard aircraft supplied to France had increased to 119 examples.

Iran (5) T-6D Standard aircraft were delivered in July 1953, and it appears that seven others had been delivered earlier in the FY50 program.

Italy (19 aircraft on hand) With a total of 20 T-6D Standard aircraft programmed, thus one still awaited. All were on hand by June 30, 1953.

Japan (20) T-6D Standard aircraft were delivered in the Third Quarter of FY55. However, all but nine of these were 'handed back' by September 30, 1956, a fact seldom recognized.

Korea (South) (30) Received 13 T-6D Standard aircraft in the 1st Quarter of FY56, and the total had reached 30 by June 30, 1956.

Norway (4) Received four T-6s under the FY50 MDAP program, but the sub-variant has not been determined. Since every other USAF MDAP T-6 aircraft for that FY was a T-6D Standard, it is fair to assume that these aircraft were T-6D Standard as well.

Portugal (20) Identified only as T-6s, but assumed to be T-6D Standard aircraft, and delivered aboard

This Brazilian Air Force Texan, S/N 1436, was supplied to the FAB under MDAP as a T-6D Standard aircraft in April 1947, along with 99 others. By the time this photo was taken, the earlier radio compass bullet and VHF mast had been replaced by a more modern, low-profile antennae. At the time of this photo, it was assigned to one of the ERA COIN squadrons. (MAP 1983-94 #31)

At least 11 T-6D Standard aircraft are visible in this view, while undergoing their upgrade for, it is believed, the Chinese Nationalist Air Force in early 1949. NAA sold at least 192 such aircraft directly to various governments. (NAA)

the USS Corregidor in October 1951.

Spain (34) of 60 T-6D Standard aircraft had been delivered by the end of FY55.

Uruguay (10) T-6D Standard aircraft were delivered in the 2nd Quarter of FY55.

In addition to the above, 30 more T-6D Standard aircraft were supplied to unknown nations under the USAF Reimbursable Aid Program between FY50 and FY54, a little-known facet of the MDAP program. An additional 50 were distributed through this program between FY54 and FY56. By FY57, not fewer than 277 T-6D Standard aircraft had been delivered under Grant Aid, yet another aspect of MDAP; they were essentially give-aways. By the end of FY59, no T-6D Standard aircraft were MDAP supported anywhere, and host-nations that had the type were left to their own devices to support the survivors.

While all of these "official" T-6D upgrades were being funneled to end-users, NAA had been busy, too. NAA had been among a crowd of bidders as early as January 1946, that had literally camped out outside the gates of Cal-Aero Field in Ontario, California. They wanted to be first in line when the War Assets Administration (WAA) put more than 200 assorted AT-6 variants on sale after cutting the asking price from $4,850 to $1,500. NAA was buying its own products back for the express purpose of selling these, after overhaul, to foreign governments not yet lucky enough to be included in any U.S. Government post-war aid programs. The scene at Cal-Aero, according to one source, was very confused, with one group actually charging that another group "ganged up on them" to prevent them from gaining first-place in line.

In January 1946, the CAA had announced that seven variants of the Texan had been approved for Group 2 certification for civil use, "after certain modifications." These variants included the BC-1A, AT-6A, AT-6B, AT-6C and former Navy SNJ-2, SNJ-3 and SNJ-4. At the beginning of 1946, at least 1,059 of these variants were in storage at 11 WAA Sales/Storage Depots, as follows:

Albuquerque, NM (272 aircraft).

Altus, OK (1 aircraft).

Augusta, GA (13 aircraft).

Camden, SC (182 aircraft).

Dos Palos, CA (56 aircraft).

Jackson, MS (52 aircraft).

Kingman, AZ (10 aircraft).

Ontario, CA (241 aircraft).

Often given as T-6Js (I believe in error), the small Data Block on a rare bird—a USAF marked, Canadian Car and Foundry Co.-built Harvard IV—actually reads just that. This is 51-17090, which was initially allotted to France, went instead went to the Italian Air Force in February 1953. It was the second Harvard IV built on U.S. MDAP contracts. (CCF via Robert F. Dorr #3055)

NORTH AMERICAN NA-16/AT-6/SNJ

T-6G-NF 49-2925, from the first batch of 371 NA-168s, is pictured in full USAF Training Command markings as worn at Hondo Field, Texas. (USAF via Robert F. Dorr)

Ponca City, OK (194 aircraft).

Vernon, TX (37 aircraft).

Walnut Ridge, AR (1 aircraft).

North American acquired at least 192 of these probably from the batch held at Ontario, California. After converting them to what they described as "roughly T-6D standard," these aircraft were sold to the national air forces of Nationalist China, Holland, Portugal and Brazil, as well as the Argentinian Navy. Subsequent sales of the "remanufactured" T-6Ds went to Chile (27 in January and February 1950), Mexico (20 in 1950), and Venezuela (20 in mid-1949). It seems likely that there were other undocumented sales. One of the key recognition features of these NAA-supplied T-6D "standard" aircraft, as opposed to those supplied via MDAP provisions, was that the RDF bullet and radio mast locations on the rear fuselage were reversed, with the bullet aft and the radio mast forward.

By July 1949, NAA was advertising a "T-6-150 model," with "more than 50 changes to meet present-day training requirements." Fuel tanks had been added in the root of each wing to provide additional capacity and extend the range to 1,000 miles; most wartime variants had a range of 629 to 665 miles. Cockpits were simplified with the instruments arranged on tilted panels. The rear cockpits were once again equipped with complete controls for instrument flight training. Radio and electronic equipment were also updated, including the addition of a VHF Command Set, range receiver, marker beacon receiver, interphone system, radio compass and an instrument approach system. The new "T-6-150" also had a steerable tail wheel. You'll quickly recognize that this is the aircraft more commonly known, to the USAF and many other users, as the T-6G.

By 1955, significant stashes of T-6s still remained around the United States. Sales to foreign nations continued, although at a diminished rate, including sales to the Dominican Republic and many others. As of January 1955, Clyde Brayton, a Dallas, Texas, broker, alone had some 83 T-6/SNJ airframes, which he confidently predicated he could "refurbish to 'D' standard and sell or exchange to foreign governments."

Before moving on to the definitive T-6G, it is instructive to examine how the USAF was using the Texans it still had on strength as of 1948. All together, the service had but 3,506 Texan variants on hand, including those assigned to Reserve components and the CAP. These were distributed as follows:

Within the Continental United States

Air Defense Command (43).

Air Materiel Command (1,265) Many of which were probably in storage.

Air Force Training Command (AFTRC) (520).

Air University (75).

Headquarters Command (12).

Strategic Air Command (46).

Tactical Air Command (98).

Air Transport Command (3).

Air Force Reserve Units (934).

Civil Air Patrol (34).

Air National Guard Units (232).

USAF ACTIVITIES OVERSEAS

Antilles Air Command (5).

Caribbean Air Command (17).

Far East Air Force (173).

Pacific Air Command (17).

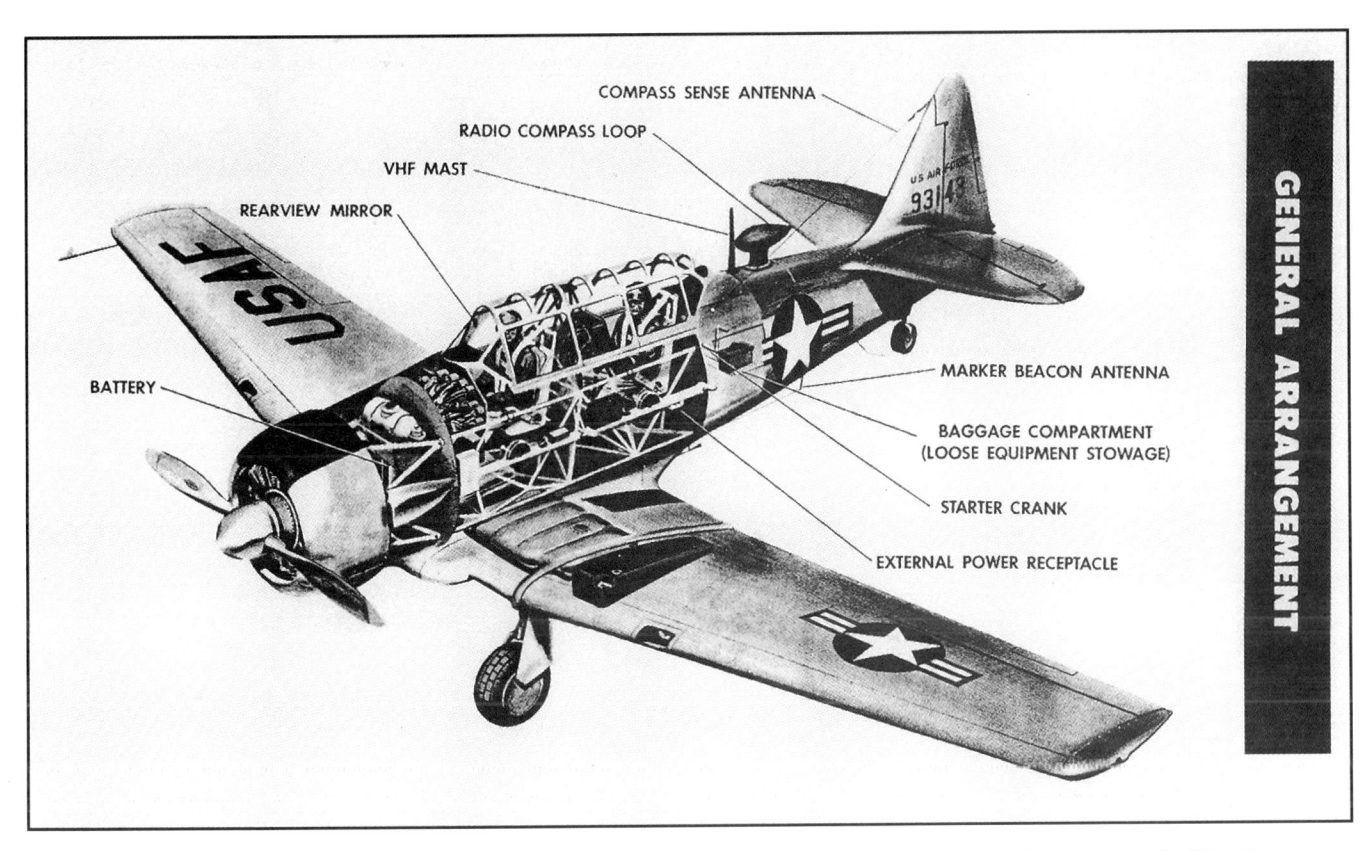

Although generally regarded as the definitive U.S. Texan variant, the five distinct batches of T-6Gs that were remanufactured for the USAF on FY 49 through FY 53 contracts actually differed significantly. This artist's concept shows the arrangement of the first NA-168 T-6G batch of 750 aircraft. (T.O. AN 01-60FFA-1)

U.S. Air Force Europe (24).

Miscellaneous Overseas Locations (6). Mainly USAF missions.

NA-168
(T-6G-NT CONTRACT AF-9212)

The first of the legendary T-6G-NTs, which were remanufactured from large batches of former AT-6 and SNJ variants, were 641 aircraft acquired by the USAF with serial numbers 49-2897 to 49-3537 (see chart).

The T-6G program had put the USAF in something of an embarrassing position. USAF no longer had the desired number of T-6/SNJ airframes on hand to provide NAA for this and subsequent contracts, so it had to buy back about 1,802 Texans (minus those already on hand), paying as much as $8,000 for aircraft that had sold surplus, in 1946 for as little as $400.

This first batch of T-6G aircraft was remanufactured specifically for issue to the USAF Training Command, and were all produced at the NAA plant at Downey, California. Of the total, 330 were remanufactured using funds that had originally been allocated for the canceled Fairchild T-31 program of 100 aircraft. The first aircraft on the T-6G contract was delivered to the Air Force just 44 days after the contract

NA-168 (T-6G-NT CONTRACT AF-9212) SERIAL NUMBERS

USAF Serials	NAA Serials
49-2897 to 49-3267	168-1 to 168-371*
49-3278 to 49-3336	168-382* to 168-440
49-3337 to 49-3386	168-451* to 168-500
49-3387 to 49-3436	168-511* to 168-560
49-3437 to 49-3486	168-571* to 168-620
49-3487 to 49-3536	168-631* to 168-680
49-3268 to 49-3277	168-681 to 168-690
49-3537	168-691

*NOTE: See the section for ANG aircraft, 50-1277 to 50-1326, to account for these Manufacturer's Serial Number discrepancies.

NORTH AMERICAN NA-16/AT-6/SNJ

Also from the initial batch of 371 T-6G-NFs, S/N 49-3129, bears the Training Command overall yellow scheme and logo on the nose. It bears the name James Connally around its upper edge in this March 1951 view. (Peter M. Bowers)

was signed. The T-6G program effectively dealt the death blow to not only the T-31, but the T-30 and T-35 from Douglas and Temco as well, although the Beech T-34 survived.

Not all T-6Gs were alike, in fact the different batches varied considerably in detail. The batch 49-2897 to 49-3537 (as well as 50-1277 to 50-1326, 51-14314 to 51-15137 and 51-17354 and subsequent aircraft) was given the RC-103 and AN/ARN-5 instrument landing system, while other series differed in the interphone systems, as such. From an armament standpoint, 49-3188 to 49-3596 and 50-1277 to 50-1326 were similarly equipped—the only non-LT-6G variants to be armament capable. While these aircraft did in fact serve Training Command, significant numbers of the survivors went on to yet third careers in the hands of foreign air arms under U.S. aid programs. Never documented before, these included the survivors listed in the chart at right.

At least 416 of this first batch of T-6Gs survived Training Command use and departed for foreign shores. An interesting anomaly: At least 45 of these aircraft were converted before deployment to the LT-6G standard.

Since the first known MDAP T-6G recipient was Portugal (20 were programmed by June 30, 1951, of which 12 had been received by that date), one or more of the Program Codes shown in the chart may have been for that destination. Other early T-6G foreign MDAP deliveries were probably also from this batch, and as of June 30, 1951, the following had been either programmed or received as shown:

France (33) 48 programmed, of which 33 had been received.

Italy (21) 30 programmed, of which 21 had been received.

Other MDAP offsets were drawn from subsequent T-6G and LT-6G batches.

NA-168 (LT-6G-NA)

The LT-6G-NA was the first aircraft actually built from the start in this new Liaison/Trainer category. These 59 remanufactured aircraft

NA-168 TRAINING COMMAND SURVIVORS

MDAP Program Code	Total	Date(s)
5T503 (Japan)	26	—
6T175 (Nicaragua)	13	Nov. 55
6T261 (Guatemala)	12	Nov. 55
6T339 (all LT-6Gs to Kimpo, Korea)	16	Apr. 57
6T340 (all LT-6Gs to Kimpo, Korea)	17	Dec. 56/Jun. 57
6T344 (unknown)	2	Dec. 56/Nov. 57
6T391 (via San Francisco)	16	Nov. 57
6T430 (Honduras)	6	Mar. 56
6T506 (France)	115	—
6T623 (via San Francisco)	17	Sep. 56
7T452 (all ex-Brookley AFB, AL)	33	57/Jan. 58
7T453 (all ex-Brookley AFB, AL)	29	Jan. 58/Jan. 59
8T276 (ex-San Francisco, an LT-6G)	1	Jan. 57
"AASBR" (all ex Davis-Monthan)	22	Jun. 57/Aug. 57
"Itabi Brindisi" (no codes, Italy?)	11	May 59/Aug. 59
Yugoslavia (no code known)	1	—
Brazil (no code known)	3	1958
Haiti (no code known)	1	Aug. 57
"2923 I" to "3324 I" (intermittent)	26	Jun. 57
(ex-San Francisco, all LT-6Gs, no code)	11	Jan. 59
(MDA, no destination codes)	38	Sep. 56/Jan. 58

received serials 49-3538 to 49-3596, and had Manufacturer's Serial Numbers 168-692 to 168-750, under Contract AF-9212. Although the Individual Aircraft Record Cards for these could not be located, they were initially destined for the USAF Training Command, but most probably ended up in Korea in 1950 to '51. The first LT-6G (S/N 49-3538) was designated as the FT-6G, which is the sole use of this unique fighter-trainer prefix.

During FY52, the peak period of the LT-6G's intense involvement in the Korean police action, the LT-6Gs flew not less than 11,063 sorties, with the high mark coming in October 1951 when 1,000 sorties were launched. Of the 81 LT-6Gs deployed in Far East Air Force units, 19 had been lost by July 1951—13 to ground fire, two to non-enemy action and four to unknown causes. By June 1952, only 63 LT-6Gs, T-6Ds and T-6Fs remained in Korea. The "Mosquitoes" had carved a truly remarkable page in U.S. Air Force history, which is unfortunately outside the scope of this book. Most of these aircraft were operated by the 6147th Tactical Air Control Squadron.

NA-168
(T-6G-NT CONTRACT AC-9212)

This supplementary contract provision was for 50 T-6Gs intended for the newly reformed state National Guard organizations. These T-6G-NTs received USAF serials 50-1277 to 50-1326 in the batches shown in the chart at right.

These aircraft came not a moment too soon. When the U.S. entered World War Two, National Guard units throughout the United States were federalized and, after the war,

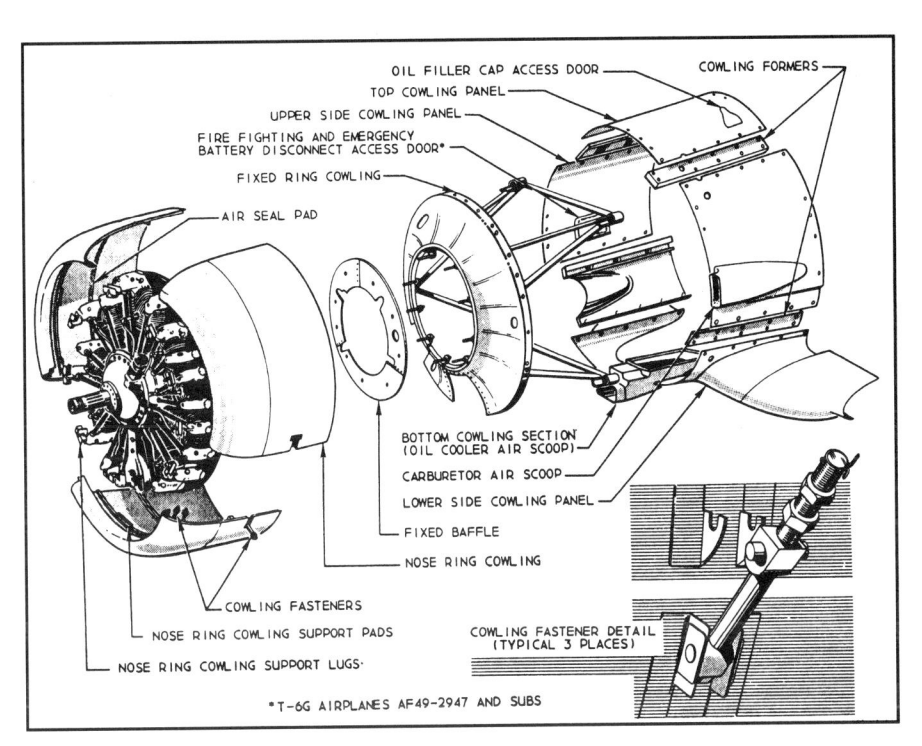

Details of the rather complex engine cowling of most T-6G series aircraft. (T.O. AN 01-60FFA-2)

considerable turmoil prevailed as the states and the active duty services struggled to rationalize the need and structure of the reconstituted National Guard air units. By May 1947, only a single AT-6 was assigned to any Air National Guard unit in the United States, increasing to four aircraft in December. By December 1948, the total still only stood at seven assorted T-6s (as they were redesignated effective 1948). The T-6Gs were ordered to partially alleviate the shortage of such aircraft, and to aid in standardization.

By 1957, even these aircraft were bound for third careers via MDAP deliveries. Of the 50 ANG T-6Gs on this contract, at least 28 went to France under project 6T506, two more to the unidentified "AASBR" project, and four others to two new projects not previously listed, three to 7T454 in November 1958 (one of which was converted to LT-6G standard) and one to Project 6T623.

NA-182
(T-6G-1-NH CONTRACT AF-21174)

In February 1951, under the impetus of the Korean police action and

NA-168 (T-6G-NT CONTRACT AC-9212) SERIAL NUMBERS

USAF Serials	Manufacturer's Serials
50-1317 to 50-1326	168-372 to 168-381
50-1277 to 50-1286	168-441 to 168-450
50-1287 to 50-1296	168-501 to 168-510
50-1297 to 50-1306	168-561 to 168-570
50-1307 to 50-1316	168-671 to 168-630

T-6G-NF49-3143 survived Training Command to go to an unspecified Mutual Defense Assistance country in 1953. (NAA via Robert F. Dorr)

the perceived Communist threat, the USAF placed one of the largest post-World War Two orders with the NAA to-date, for not fewer than 824 T-6Gs to be remanufactured at the new Columbus, Ohio, facility. These were given USAF serials 51-14314 to 51-15137 (NAA Serials 182-1 to 182-824, in straight-forward sequence for a change).

The vast majority of initial shipments went to the Air Training Command facility at Columbus, Missouri, beginning in May 1952. By May 1955, however, MDAP offsets had begun from this large batch. At least 138 went to MDAP users, including Iran, France, Nicaragua, Greece, Yugoslavia, Honduras, Guatemala, Bolivia and several unidentified destinations. At least 29 of these were converted to the LT-6G configuration prior to shipment. Thus, together with earlier T-6G blocks, by June 30, 1953, distribution of MDAP T-6G aircraft looked like this:

France (48 aircraft).

Italy (30 aircraft).

Portugal (20 aircraft).

A year later, however, MDAP offsets had increased in tempo, and the situation looked like this as of June 30, 1954:

France (62 aircraft).

Italy (30) Unchanged at 30 T-6Gs.

Portugal (20) Unchanged at 20 T-6Gs.

Stenciling on most T-6Gs was extensive, and this close-up of T-6G-NF S/N 50-1290 of the California National Guard, taken in July 1951, is typical. This aircraft later went to the French Air Force under MAP Project 6T506. (William T. Larkins via David W. Ostrowski)

Ramp scene at the NAA Columbus, Ohio, facility, the old Curtiss-Wright factory where many of the T-6Gs were remanufactured, as it looked in November 1951 (NAA)

Greece (17 aircraft) All delivered in the second quarter of FY55.

Iran (23 LT-6Gs) Of 36 due by the end of the third quarter, FY55.

Japan (45 T-6Gs) All due by the end of the third quarter FY55.

By June 30, 1955, MDAP T-6G deliveries had more or less settled into their final form, with minor subsequent variations. The totals looked like this:

France (62 delivered) Final total, all Grant Aid. By June 30, 1958, the number of these that were MAP supported had dropped to 37.

Italy (30 delivered) Final total, all Grant Aid.

Portugal (20 delivered) Final total, all Grant Aid. By December 31, 1957, only 16 were still MAP supported, and that was the last entry for MAP support.

Greece (17 delivered). Final total, all Grant Aid. However, between September 1957 and June 1958, the number on hand increased from 16 to 28, all MAP supported.

Iran (36 LT-6Gs delivered) A final total of 40 was achieved by September 30, 1956, all Grant Aid, but this had increased to 45 LT-6Gs MAP supported by June 1958.

Turkey (3 T-6Gs programmed for FY56) A final total of 19 LT-6Gs was achieved by September 30, 1956, all Grant Aid. By September 1957, 30 T-6Gs were MAP supported, but no LT-6Gs.

Japan (45 T-6Gs delivered) A final total of 110 was achieved by September 30, 1956, all Grant Aid. However, by March 31, 1958, not less than 175 were MAP-supported, the last date so shown.

Philippines (8) Although 25 were due by June 30, 1956, apparently only eight were received by June 30, 1957, all Grant Aid.

Thailand (74) An unspecified quantity was programmed, but the first report of any actually on hand was September 1957, when 74 had been delivered.

Vietnam (18) An unspecified quantity was programmed. However,

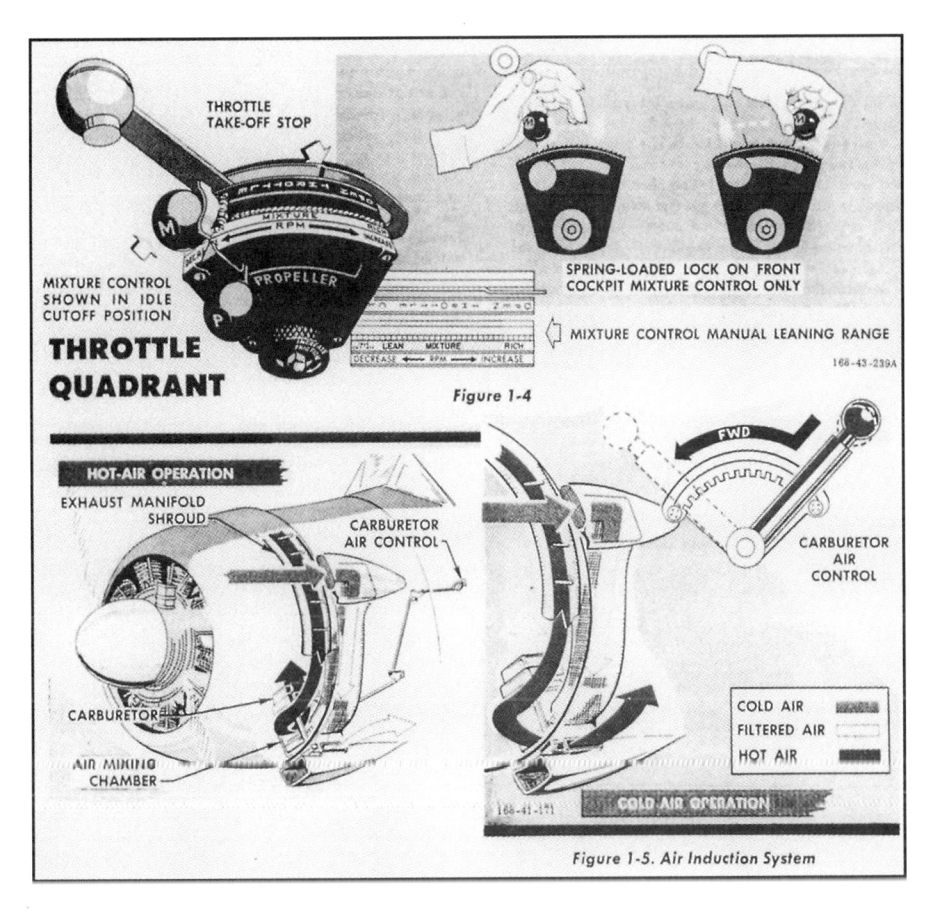

Details of the basic T-6G throttle quadrant and carburetor air controls. (T.O. AN 01-60FFA-1)

The solitary FT-6G, S/N 49-3538, precursor of the LT-6G, was a standard T-6G-NF. The fate of this aircraft is unknown. (via Robert F. Dorr)

A frontal view of the one-and-only FT-6G, S/N 49-3538, shows the arrangement of the four 100-pound bombs, two .30-caliber gun pods and a ferry tank. (via Robert F. Dorr)

LT-6G-NF, S/N 49-3558, was shot down by enemy ground fire over the North on August 17, 1955, but was recovered. It is not clear if it was rebuilt or not. (via Robert F. Dorr)

Ordered initially for issuance primarily to Air Guard units, the 824 NA-182s saw widespread distribution to MDAP recipients after USAF and ANG use. Here, S/N 51-14337 is shown as it appeared in 1953. The Crew Chief is named in the wing under the front cockpit as A2C H.J. Sack! (Leo J. Kohn)

none had materialized until December 31, 1957, when 18 were on-hand.

Chile (23) An unspecified quantity was programmed, and 10 were received by June 30, 1957, all Grant Aid. This number had increased to 23 by September 1957.

Uruguay (10) An unspecified quantity was programmed, and 10 were received by the fourth quarter of FY57, all Grant Aid.

Spain (60) Did not have any T-6Gs, MAP-supported or otherwise, until March 31, 1958, when not less than 60 were on strength

Ecuador (7) Had received seven MAP-supported T-6Gs by September 1957.

NA-186
(T-6J AND CCF HARVARD IV)

A great deal of confusion has surrounded the alleged use of the USAF designation T-6J to cover the MDAP-procured Harvard IV aircraft that were built as new aircraft by the Canadian Car and Foundry Co., Ltd. These were the only variants built as totally new aircraft postwar.

It is true the USAF planned to acquire a quantity of developments of the T-6G, to be built at the NAA Columbus, Ohio, plant as T-6Js on Contract AF-25930 (dated June 22, 1951). However, this contract was terminated, and the basic design data was sold to CCF. Over the intervening years, the alleged use of this designation in connection with the Harvard IV has gained currency, but it is apparently completely without foundation. I made a complete review of every single Individual Aircraft History Cards for the Harvard IV aircraft that was built under MDAP contracts (and assigned U.S. serials as a consequence), and there is not a single reference to the designation T-6J on any of these. In the block where the designation is typically entered on these cards, the type was given as Harvard IV in every case. The RCAF aircraft were properly cited as Harvard 4s from the start, but this presentation of the Mark number is unique to the RCAF examples only.

The 285 Harvard IVs built and given U.S. serial numbers were all for MDAP delivery. It is seldom noted that CCF also built an additional 270 for the RCAF (RCAF serials 20210 to 20479, Mfg. S/N CCF4-1 to CCF4-270), and these are hardly ever included in totals for the series. Some of the RCAF aircraft, following the acceptance of the first example in November 1951, served as late as August 1967 and beyond. Thirty-six of them passed to the Indian Air Force in 1963, while 56 others gained Canadian civil registrations after surplusing. At least six of these aircraft are noted in RCAF records as "returned to USAF after loan" in 1953. It is just possible that these are the aircraft that may have gained the designation T-6J, but I could locate no record of their disposition, nor are any Individual Aircraft Record Cards for serial numbers known. James Fahey's handy booklet entitled "USAF Aircraft 1947-1956" (Ships and Aircraft, Falls Church, Virginia, 1956) lists it as "T-6J-CC" and states that there were some "50 plus aircraft by Can-Car for MSP," which at least gives a period source. It is little-known that, while the RCAF was awaiting the delivery of their new CCF-built Harvard 4s, they borrowed 100 T-6Ds between May 12, 1951, and February 1954, operating them with their USAF serials. Six of these aircraft were lost during their RCAF sojourn, and in a unique arrangement, were replaced in 1952 by Harvard 4s built for the RCAF.

The first batch of 143 Harvard IVs under Contract AF-20641 were assigned U.S. serials 51-17089 to 51-17231 (CCF serials CCF4-271 to CCF4-413). Of these, 67 went to the

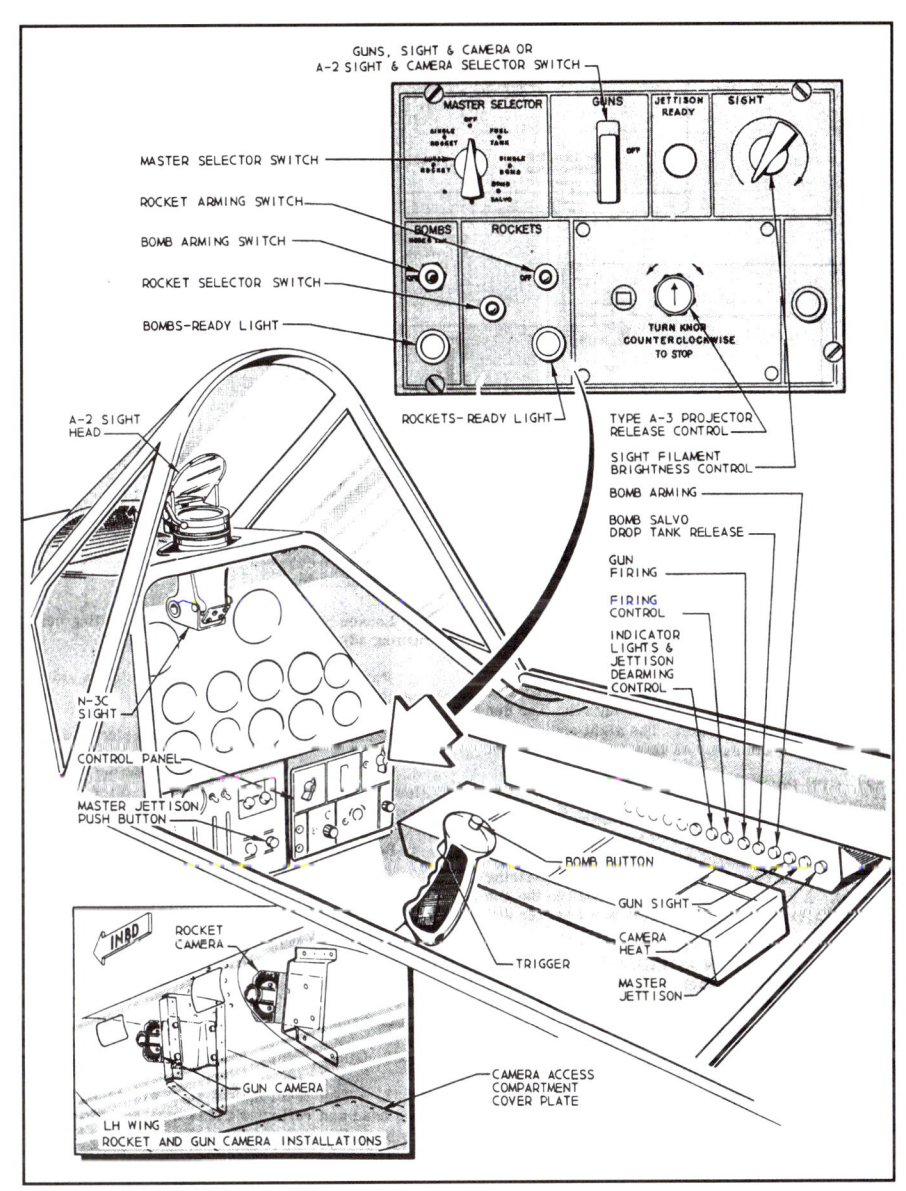

Layout of the cockpit gunnery and underwing ordnance controls in the LT-6G, as of February 1952. (T.O. AN 01-60FFA-2)

The 110 T-6G-NFs (NA-197s) were remanufactured exclusively for issue to Air National Guard units, such as S/N 52-8206 of the Wisconsin ANG shown here at Milwaukee on May 16, 1953. This aircraft later went to the French Air Force under MDA Project 6T506. (Leo J. Kohn)

Italian Air Force between February and September 1953, 24 to the Belgian Air Force during the same period, and the remainder of 51 aircraft went to the French Air Force.

The second batch of 120 aircraft (U.S. serials 52-8493 to 52-8612, Mfg. S/N CCF4-414 to CCF4-533) went entirely to the newly reconstituted West German Air Force, split between Landsberg and Erding air bases in December 1956. Except the very first two, which went to the Italian Air Force.

The final batch of just 22 aircraft (U.S. serials 53-4615 to 53-4636, Mfg. S/N CCF4-534 to CCF4-555), built by the CCF facility at Fort William, Ontario, all went to the West German Air Force, also in December 1956. These aircraft had the distinction of gaining the "highest" serial number sequence of any U.S.-funded Texan/Harvard series aircraft. The delivery was split, like the earlier WGAF aircraft, between Erding and Landsberg air bases.

While it is often stated that the Harvard IV was built "to T-6G standard," this is somewhat misleading, as a detailed examination of an aircraft of each type would quickly reveal. Some of the aircraft (e.g., RCAF 20293) had T-6G-style canopy framing, but earlier examples (e.g., RCAF 20248) had the old, war-time AT-6D style framing. One commonality, and a usually reliable recognition feature, was the radio mast immediately aft of the segmented rearmost canopy section and the "flat" or small style ADF mounting just astern of that. They also had an exhaust shroud on the right-hand side of the fuselage. Some later aircraft had a radio mast on top of the rear-most canopy frame and a large tear-drop ADF loop on a pedestal on the upper-mid-rear fuselage.

NA-188 (T-6G-NH AND T-6G-NA)

In April 1951, the USAF ordered two additional batches of T-6Gs on Contract AF-24716. One hundred went out for Mutual Defense Assistance assignment from the Dallas facility (51-15138 to 51-15237, Mfg. S/N 188-1 to 188-100, of which NAA furnished 60 from its own resources on

A Missouri ANG T-6G-NF, S/N 52-8232 with (probably) a red prop spinner, fin tip and wing tips. (Robert Esposito via David W. Ostrowski)

S.O. 3912), and seven others came from the NAA Downey, California, facility, also for MDAP (51-16071 to 51-16077, Mfg. S/N 188-101 to 188-107). The larger of these two groups almost certainly figure into the distributions to foreign nations shown in the preceding section. However, not a single Individual Aircraft History Card for this series could be found, consequently, their deployment is not documented. The smaller group of seven was initially assigned (despite the funding citation) to USAF training activities, possibly training foreign cadets at Hondo, Texas. Of the seven, three eventually did go to MDAP assignments: one each to Honduras, Guatemala and Nicaragua between November 1955 and March 1956. Most of these aircraft were remanufactured AT-6Bs and AT-6Cs.

A recapitulation of T-6G MAP-supported aircraft, as of September 30, 1958, shows how these additional aircraft may have been deployed, beyond those deliveries already reflected in earlier batches. MAP-supported T-6Gs, LT-6Gs and RLT-6Gs looked like this by that date:

France (37 T-6Gs).

Spain (60 T-6Gs).

Greece (28 T-6Gs) Increased to 52 by June 30, 1958.

Iran (4 RLT-6Gs and 44 LT-6Gs).

Pakistan (41 T-6Gs).

Turkey (30 T-6Gs, and by June 30, 1958, 19 LT-6Gs).

Cambodia (12 Grant Aid LT-6Gs) Received by March 31, 1959.

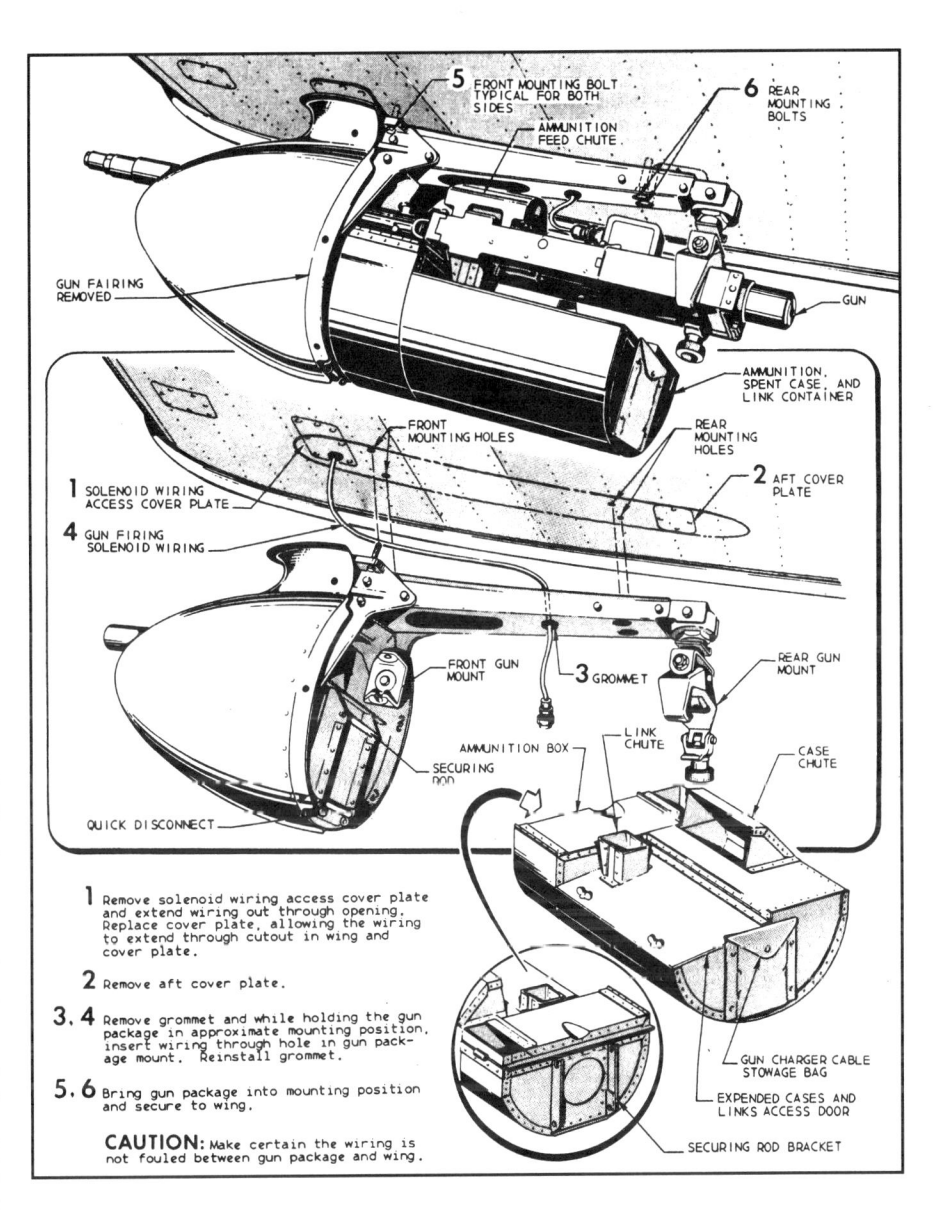

Details of the .30-caliber machine gun package as used on the LT-6Gs, and later on some foreign T-6 variants that were supplied under MDAP and MAP. (T.O. AN 01-60FFA-2)

South Korea (24 LT-6Gs) Received by December 31, 1958.

Philippines (8 T-6Gs).

Thailand (74 T-6Gs).

South Vietnam (18 Grant Aid T-6Gs).

Chile (19 T-6Gs) 10 of them Grant Aid.

Cuba (2 T-6Gs) For which MAP support, significantly, ended on December 31, 1958.

Ecuador (7 T-6Gs).

Uruguay (10 T-6Gs).

By 1962, these nations had been joined by Laos, with 8 T-6Gs, and the Dominican Republic, 26 T-6Gs, which was apparently the last nation to receive the type under MAP.

NORTH AMERICAN NA-16/AT-6/SNJ

ANG T-6Gs were common sights during the early 1950s, and this Washington ANG example, S/N 53-4589 was one of the last 60 NA-197s. Note the "Ace of Spades" insignia on the forward fuselage, just visible behind the pitot head cover, as of May 1, 1954. This aircraft, like many others, later went to the French Air Force under MDA Project 6T506. (Peter M. Bowers)

NA-195 (T-6G-NA)

Yet another small batch of 11 aircraft were ordered as remanufactured aircraft from the NAA Fresno facility in March 1952, coded on Contract AF-15912 as being for Mutual Defense.

These aircraft (USAF S/N 51-17354 to 51-17364, Mfg. S/N 196-1 to 195-11) were instead distributed throughout the USAF training establishment, apparently as replacement aircraft. Examples went to Luke, Bainbridge, Hondo,

Even the midwestern Iowa ANG received T-6Gs from the last batch, such as S/N 53-4602, which was the 12th from last T-6 to receive a U.S. serial number. This aircraft also went to an unknown MDA country in December 1956, possibly Brazil. (Leo J. Kohn)

The ultimate U.S. Navy Texan variant was the SNJ-7, an indeterminate number of which were remanufactured for the Navy by NAA roughly to a mix of T-6F and T-6G standard. This example (Bu. No. 112229) received the "B" suffix, indicating a number of special features (including armament capability). It was photographed at Saufley Field on February 24, 1954, while assigned to BTU-2. (James Fahey via David W. Ostrowski)

1. Right Tank Low Fuel Quantity Warning Light
2. Directional Gyro
3. Gyro Horizon Indicator
4. Manifold Pressure Gage
5. Rate-of-Climb Indicator
6. Carburetor Mixture Temperature Indicator
7. Free Air Temperature Indicator
8. Ammeter
9. Tachometer
10. Cylinder Head Temperature Indicator
11. Engine Gage Unit—Fuel and Oil Pressure and Oil Temperature
12. Pilot's Check List
13. Clock
14. Sight Rheostat
15. Jettison-ready Light
16. Fuel-tank-ready Light
17. Gun Selector Switch
18. Master Selector Switch
19. Rocket Projector Release Control
20. Primer
21. Rocket Arming Switch
22. Rocket Projector Release Control Indicator
23. Rockets-ready Light
24. Drop Tank Emergency Jettison Handle
25. Rocket Selector Switch
26. Bomb Arming Switch
27. Bombs-ready Light
28. Parking Brake Handle
29. Accelerometer
30. Altimeter
31. Master Jettison Button
32. Landing Gear Downlock Indicator Lights
33. Landing Gear Position Indicators
34. Wing Flap Position Indicator
35. Landing Light Switches
36. Hydraulic Pressure Gage
37. Remote-indicating Compass Indicator
38. Suction Gage
39. Ignition Switch
40. Radio Compass Indicator
41. Stand-by Compass
42. Marker Beacon Indicator Light
43. Turn-and-Bank Indicator
44. Airspeed Indicator
45. Drop Tank Shutoff Switch
46. Drop Tank Low Fuel Quantity Warning Light
47. Left Tank Low Fuel Quantity Warning Light

The front office of the LT-6G shows the instrument array. (T.O. AN 01-60FFD-1)

NORTH AMERICAN
NA-16/AT-6/SNJ

This post-war AT-6F, S/N 44-81821, photographed in California in 1947, has some form of "nose art" on the forward fuselage, probably for recruiting. (Leo J. Kohn)

A number of T-6Fs saw service in the Korean war, including this otherwise anonymous example, which sits next to what appears to be a camouflaged example. (David W. Ostrowski)

San Marcos and principally to Bartow. None were dispersed under MDAP, and survivors ended their days at Davis-Monthan AFB until being surplused.

NA-197 (T-6G-NF)

The final two batches of USAF-procured T-6Gs, consisting of lots of 50 and 60 aircraft (52-8197 to 52-8246, Mfg. S/N 197-1 to 197-50, and 53-4555 to 53-4614, Mfg. S/N 197-51 to 197-110) were ordered on Contract AF-20914 (and Supplement 1) dated June 16, 1952. This work was accomplished at Fresno, and consisted of the remanufacture of previously remanufactured National Guard T-6D Standard aircraft.

Of these two batches, every single example in the first batch of 50 went to MDAP, at least 24 to France. Of the last group of 60, not fewer than 49 went to MDAP destinations, including 29 to France. At least four from this batch were converted to LT-6G configuration before deployment.

At least 411 USAAF AT-6Fs transferred to the Navy were designated SNJ-6. Here, Bu. No. 112318 poses in 1947 with a snazzy anti-glare panel detailing job and similar work to the prop spinner, plus a lot of polish on the airframe. It was assigned to NAS Alameda at the time, later serving with VT-1A and BTU-1. It was overhauled at Pensacola in August 1949. (Leo J. Kohn)

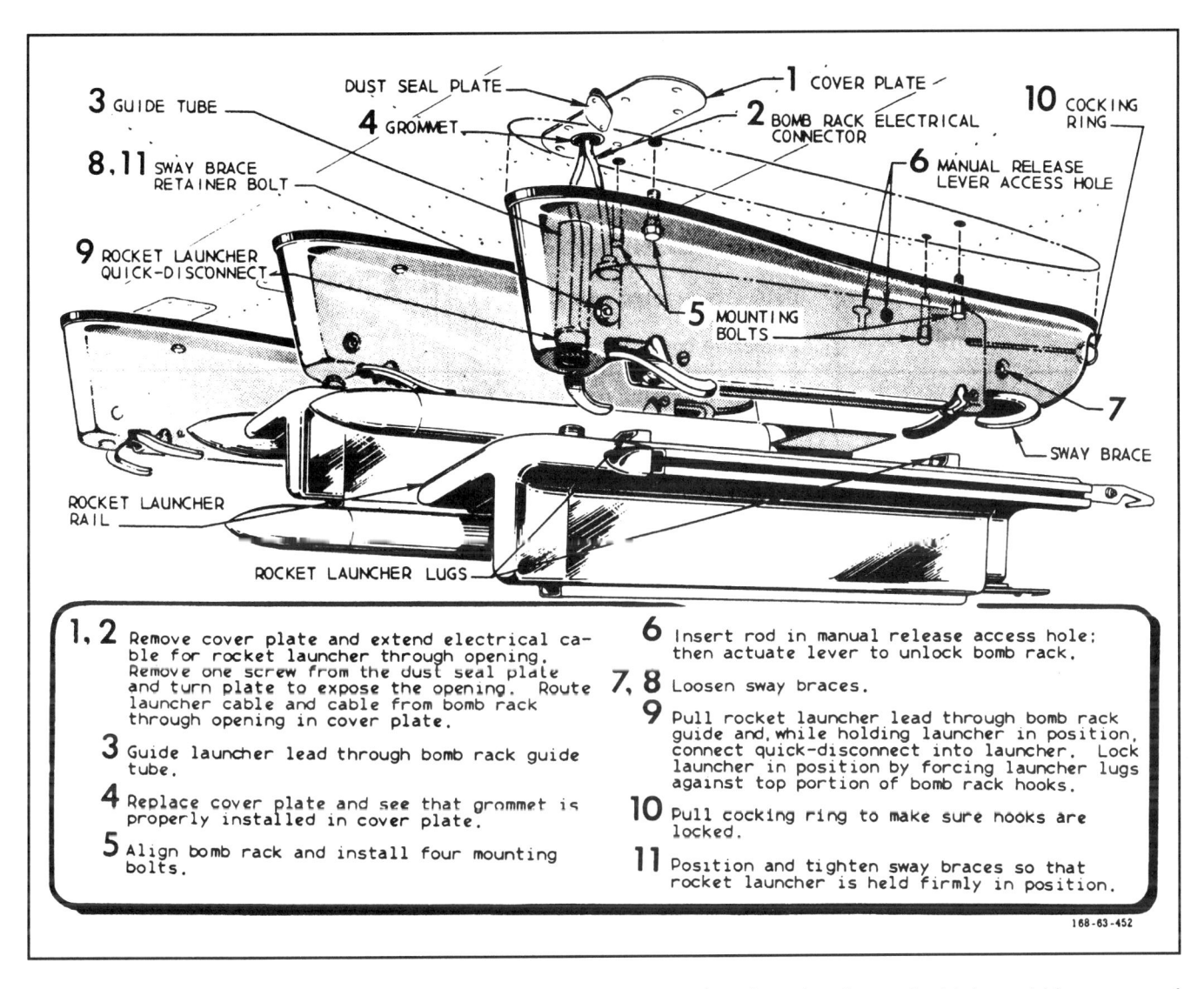

In addition to accommodating gun packs, the inboard Type S-2 bomb racks, three of which could be mounted under each wing, held a special 2.25-Inch rocket launcher adapter, as shown here. This proved to be one of the most oft-used installations in Korea. (T.O. AN 01-60FFA-2)

SNJ-7

Oddly, although the U.S. Navy planned to upgrade as many as 50 mixed early SNJ variants to T-6G-like standard at Pensacola, apparently with kits acquired from Columbus, only six were actually known to have been converted. These included a single SNJ-7 (Bu. No. 112383), two SNJ-7B gunnery trainers (Bu. No. 27850 and 12229) and three SNJ-7Cs with arrestor gear (Bu. No. 90678, 90743 and 112314). These eventually ended up with very nonstandard Navy designations that reflected their former series numbers and experimental status, including SNJ-4-7BX, SNJ-5-7X and SNJ-6-7CX. As these were not NAA products, they had no NAA Charge Number other than that under which they had originally been built.

NA-198 (SNJ-8)

What would have been the last U.S. service order for Texan variants for American use was a U.S. Navy order for 240 SNJ-8s placed July 3, 1952. Similar to the T-6G, though, this entire order was canceled. They would have become Bu. No. 137246 to 137485 (Mfg. S/N 198-1 to 198-240). It was forecast that they would have eventually received the designation TJ-8.

RLT-6G

Now for a batch of rather mysterious aircraft, which sharp-eyed readers will have noted earlier in this account. Commencing in Fiscal Year 1957 documents, the USAF reported that it was supporting 46 LT-6Gs and four RLT-6Gs in the inventory

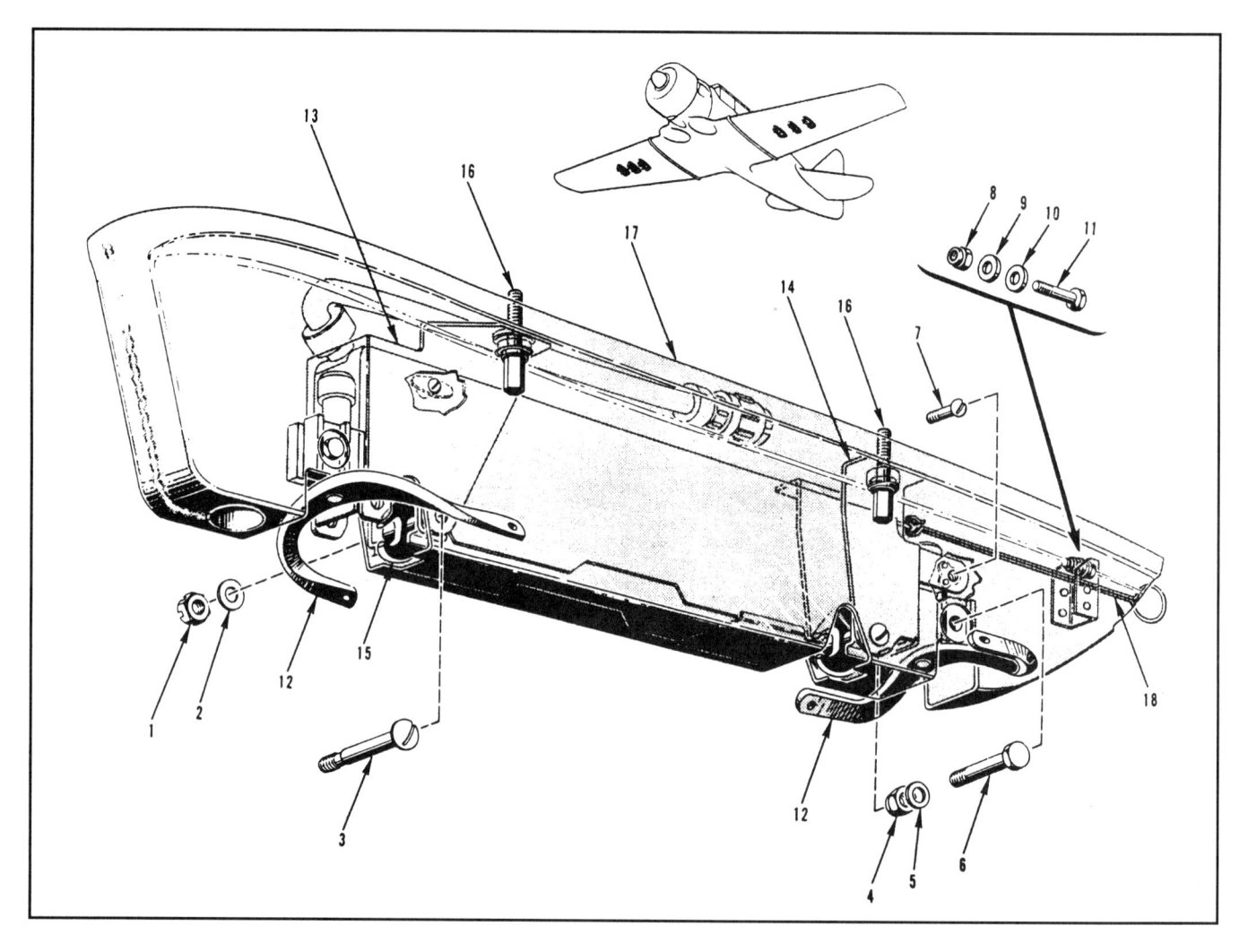

One of the special Type S-2 bomb rack (NAA Part No. 168-63012) assemblies in detail, three of which could be fitted under each wing of the LT-6G. (T.O. AN 01-60FFA-4)

of the Imperial Iranian Air Force. By June 30, 1960, MAP was still supporting 33 conventional LT-6Gs in Iran and a single RLT-6G.

Despite intensive efforts, I have been utterly unable to define the significance of these four aircraft, nor what modifications justified the "R" prefix to the conventional designation.

OTHER POST-WAR TEXANS

Throughout this account, I have made an effort to illustrate how truly universal the distribution of T-6 variants became after the end of World War Two. While the U.S. and British aid program offsets and surplus sales directly to other nations account for a large number of aircraft, it is by no means the complete story.

Likewise, a number of specialized modifications on T-6 variants were undertaken by firms in Belgium, France, Spain and Portugal—usually involving armament—but also the addition of specialized equipment, such as the extra oil cooler intake atop the cowlings on many French Air Force aircraft used in North Africa. The Spanish Air Force went so far as to designate some of their modified aircraft in the "C" for Caza (fighter) designation series as C.6s. These had two 7.7MM wing guns and provisions for 10-kilogram bombs or rockets.

Besides the nations otherwise represented in this account, the following nations also acquired Texans:

Indonesian Air Force (15) Acquired approximately 15 T-6s of unknown variants from the United States via arms dealers between 1951-1955.

Nationalist Chinese Air Force (Taiwan/Formosa) (12) Acquired at least 12 T-6s from the United States via unknown sources in 1951.

Indian Air Force (30) Reliably

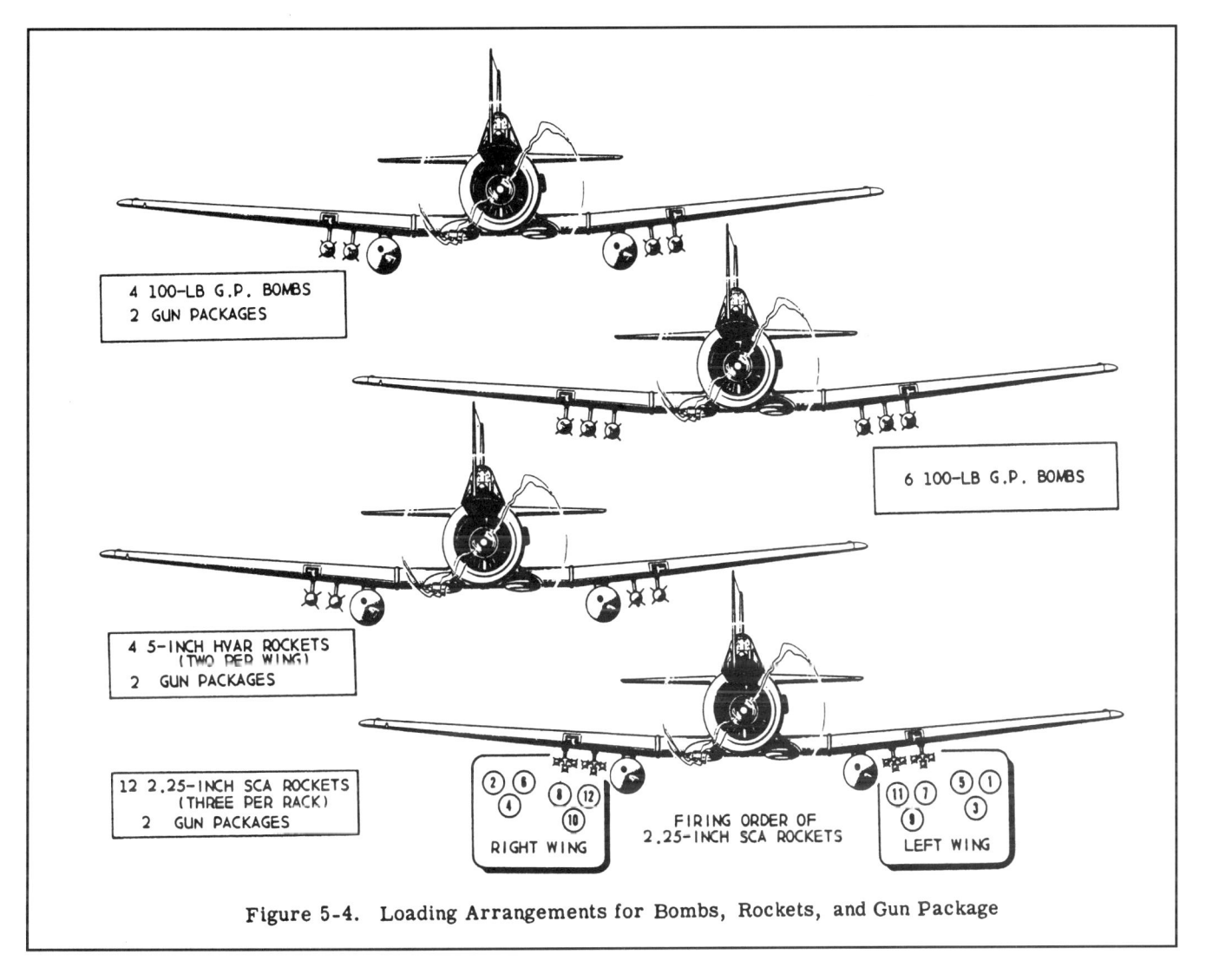

Figure 5-4. Loading Arrangements for Bombs, Rockets, and Gun Package

The LT-6G could accommodate four standard ordnance loading arrangements. (T.O. AN 01-60FFA-2)

reported to have acquired 30 T-6Gs from the United States in 1956, possibly via one of the "unidentified" MAP project numbers reported earlier.

Egyptian Air Force (15) Acquired 15 ex-Royal Canadian Air Force Harvard IIBs in 1955.

Iraqi Air Force (6) Acquired six Harvard IIBs from British stocks in 1951.

Israeli Defense Force/Air Force (21) Acquired a mix of at least 21 T-6 variants from U.S. sources starting in 1950.

Syrian Air Force (5) Acquired at least five RAF surplus Harvards in 1954.

Yemani Air Force (2) Acquired two of the former Saudi Arabian T-6s in 1955, which became part of the Imam's private fleet of aircraft.

Moroccan Air Force (50) Received 50 T-6 variants from the U.S. prior to 1964, possibly under some of the untraced MAP project numbers.

Tunisian Air Force (12) Received 12 ex-French Air Force T-6 variants in 1963.

Zaire/Congolese Air Force (16) Acquired two Harvards from the Belgian firm COGEA in 1961, which were originally intended for Katanqa, but were diverted. They also acquired two former Belgian Air Force machines in 1963, and 12 ex-Italian Air Force T-6Gs in 1964. An attempt to acquire 20 more T-6s in the United States during 1964-65 is vague, and it is not clear if any arrived or not from this batch. The break-away province of Katanga is often credited with acquiring eight ex-Belgian T-6s in 1961 and 11 more in 1962, but this is problematical.

SIGNIFICANT DATES

KEY DATES IN THE HISTORY OF THE NA-16/AT-6/SNJ

1 APRIL 1935
Eddie Allen, later to become famous as the test pilot killed while flying an early Boeing B-29, pilots the first flight of the number one NA-16, X-2080, at Dundalk, Maryland.

3 OCTOBER 1935
NAA scores its first production order for 42 BT-9 basic trainers based on the NA-16 for the U.S. Army Air Corps. It is followed by a second order for 40 BT-9As for issue to Air Corps Reserve units.

15 APRIL 1936
P. Balfour makes the first flight of a production Army Air Corps BT-9.

20 OCTOBER 1936
The NA-26 prototype, NAA entry in the new Air Corps Basic Combat Trainer competition, Proposal 37-220, is launched. It is the true progenitor of the later AT-6, as it features a Pratt & Whitney R-1340 engine, armament and for the first time retractable landing gear identical to later production versions.

1 DECEMBER 1936
A follow-up order for 117 BT-9Bs is received for the Army Air Corps.

1 DECEMBER 1936
NAA achieves its first export success, selling the single NA-27 (NA-16-2H) Basic Combat Trainer to Fokker in the Netherlands as the "European Demonstrator." The aircraft gains Dutch registration PH-APG and is later impressed into the Royal Dutch Army Air Force to become one of the first NAA products to fall to enemy action when it was destroyed on the ground in Holland on May 11, 1940.

14 DECEMBER 1936
The U.S. Navy gets on the NAA bandwagon with an order for 40 NJ-1s, basically a variant of the BT-9 that had been modified for Navy requirements.

22 DECEMBER 1936
Momentum grows in production as NAA receives additional follow-on orders from the Air Corps for 66 BT-9Cs for issue, initially, to Air Corps Reserve units. A single Y1BT-10 is included in this contract.

8 FEBRUARY 1937
NAA scores its first sale to a foreign air arm when Sweden's Royal Air Force acquires a single NA-31 (NA-16-4M), which is basically similar to the BT-9 but with a different engine. This is also the first sale of Manufacturing Rights to a foreign country.

10 MARCH 1937
Close on the heels of the Swedish contract, NAA sells single examples of the NA-32 (NA-16-1A) and NA-33 (NA-16-2K) to Australia, along with manufacturing rights for both. The latter becomes the Commonwealth Wirraway, the first NAA NA-16 derivative to see combat and possibly the only variant to score an air-to-air kill.

19 MARCH 1937
Although single examples of NA-16 series aircraft had been exported previously with manufacturing rights, the first production export order comes, significantly, from a Western Hemisphere nation, Argentina, which orders 30 NA-34s (NA-16-4Ps) for its Army Aviation Command. These remain in service well into the 1950s, long after other NA-16 variants had been retired by major powers.

16 JUNE 1937
The Army Air Corps orders 177 BC-1 Basic Combat Trainers based on the earlier NA-26 entry.

9 DECEMBER 1937
The Central American nation of Honduras acquires the former NA-20 (NA-16-2H) demonstrator, modified, as well as two new NA-42 (NA-16-2A) combat aircraft, which one the first truly modern aircraft of this type in Central America.

9 DECEMBER 1937
The first NA-44 Light Attack Bomber is originated. This is a direct descendant of the large number of Harvard aircraft ordered by the British Commonwealth of Nations, and the aircraft is itself sold to the Royal Canadian Air Force in 1940 after a successful export sales tour of Latin America.

7 FEBRUARY 1938
The British Royal Air Force orders 400 NA-49s (NA-16-1E, in two batches of 200 each) as Harvard I trainers.

11 FEBRUARY 1938
The first flight of a USAAC BC-1 is made by P. Balfour.

23 FEBRUARY 1938
The Chinese Nationalist Government orders 35 NA-41s (NA-16-4s), which is essentially the same as the USAAC BT-9C. This is NAA's second significant export order.

1 AUGUST 1938
The first single-seat fighter derivative of the NA-16, the NA-50, is procured by Peru, with a total of seven acquired.

23 SEPTEMBER 1938
The U.S. Navy orders 16 SNJ-1s in the new "Scout Trainer" category, which are similar to the NA-36 (BC-1) but incorporate the improvements of the NA-44.

28 SEPTEMBER 1938
The first Harvard I is flown for the first time by L.S. Walt.

21 FEBRUARY 1939
With war clouds once again on the horizon, France places an order for 230 NA-57s, which are similar to the USAAC BT-9B), the largest single order to date for NAA.

23 APRIL 1939
The USAAC orders 251 BT-14 basic trainers, the largest domestic order for an NA-16 variant as of that date. These were essentially similar to the NA-23, but incorporated improvements pioneered in the NA-55. They were the last fixed-gear NAA variants for the U.S. military. On the same date, the USAAC ordered 94 AT-6s, which was essentially a continuation of an NA-55 (BC-1A) contract merely changing the Basic Combat trainer designation to Advanced Trainer.

3 JANUARY 1940
L.S. Wait makes the first flight of an USAAC BT-14.

6 FEBRUARY 1940
L.S. Wait flies the first flight of an AT-6.

24 JUNE 1940
The U.S. Navy orders 25 SNJ-2s (NA-79s).

28 JUNE 1940
The USAAC orders not less than 517 AT-6As (NA-77), concurrent with a USN order for 120 identical SNJ-3s. Subsequent orders increased AT-6A orders by 1,330, and of SNJ-3s by 150.

6 DECEMBER 1940
The USAAC orders 400 AT-6Bs (NA-84s) as armament trainers. These become the first U.S. NA-16 variants to gain the name Texan on the production line. These are also the first variants to be built entirely at the Dallas, Texas, facility.

10 APRIL 1941
Initial orders are placed by the USAAC for an eventual total of not fewer than 9,331 AT-6C, AT-6D, SNJ-4 and SNJ-5 advanced trainers (NA-88s).

11 FEBRUARY 1944
The final wartime USAAF contract is let for 800 AT-6Ds and 956 AT-6Fs, although the contract was reduced from 2,175 airplanes, and reduced further later on.

5 OCTOBER 1949
The USAF contracts for an initial batch of remanufactured T-6Gs and LT-6Gs for issuance to Air Training Command and National Guard units totaling 750 aircraft, giving a new lease on life to many wartime variants that were upgraded to this standard. Subsequent orders followed, totaling an additional 1,052 aircraft.

3 JULY 1953
The very last contract for an NA-16 descendant is for 240 SNJ-8s for the U.S. Navy, but the contract is cancelled in its entirety as events overtake the requirement.